1997

DWELLING CONSTRUCTION UNDER THE UNIFORM BUILDING CODE™

INTERNATIONAL CONFERENCE OF BUILDING OFFICIALS · 1922 ·
UNIFORM BUILDING CODE ®

First Printing

Publication Date: May 1998

ISBN 1-58001-005-9

International Conference of Building Officials
5360 WORKMAN MILL ROAD
WHITTIER, CALIFORNIA 90601-2298
(800) 284-4406 • (562) 699-0541

PRINTED IN THE U.S.A.

Preface

This publication is for the convenience of the home builder who is interested in building a house in conformance with the Building Code. The material conforms to the 1997 edition of the *Uniform Building Code*™ (UBC), which is dedicated to the development of better building construction and greater safety to the public.

The standards of safe construction that are set out in the *Uniform Building Code* are founded primarily upon health and safety but will, at the same time, protect the owner's investment. By following the requirements in this publication, the home builder will gain the double satisfaction of complying with the law and also securing a dwelling of sound and durable construction.

The *Uniform Building Code,* from which this material is taken, is comprehensive and flexible so that no material or method of construction that is permanent and safe is excluded. Consequently, there are construction materials and practices that are permitted but which are not mentioned herein because of the limitations and purposes of this publication.

The subject matter applies only to the construction of one- or two-story dwellings of wood stud wall construction. The building official should be consulted for information on different types of construction. The sections and tables referred to will be found in the 1997 edition of the *Uniform Building Code.*

Parenthetical references following the various sections of this publication refer to the section of the *Uniform Building Code* in which the requirement may be found.

CODES AND RELATED PUBLICATIONS

The International Conference of Building Officials (ICBO) publishes a family of codes, each correlated with the *Uniform Building Code™* to provide jurisdictions with a complete set of building-related regulations for adoption. Some of these codes are published in affiliation with other organizations such as the International Fire Code Institute (IFCI) and the International Code Council (ICC). Reference materials and related codes also are available to improve knowledge of code enforcement and administration of building inspection programs. Publications and products are continually being added, so inquiries should be directed to Conference headquarters for a listing of available products. Many codes and references are also available on CD-ROM or floppy disk. These are denoted by (*). The following publications and products are available from ICBO:

CODES

***Uniform Building Code**, Volumes 1, 2 and 3. The most widely adopted model building code in the United States, the performance-based *Uniform Building Code* is a proven document, meeting the needs of government units charged with the enforcement of building regulations. Volume 1 contains administrative, fire- and life-safety and field inspection provisions; Volume 2 contains structural engineering design provisions; and Volume 3 contains material, testing and installation standards.

***Uniform Mechanical Code™.** Provides a complete set of requirements for the design, construction, installation and maintenance of heating, ventilating, cooling and refrigeration systems; incinerators and other heat-producing appliances.

International Plumbing Code™. Provides consistent and technically advanced requirements that can be used across the country to provide comprehensive regulations of modern plumbing systems. Setting minimum regulations for plumbing facilities in terms of performance objectives, the IPC provides for the acceptance of new and innovative products, materials and systems.

International Private Sewage Disposal Code™. Provides flexibility in the development of safety and sanitary individual sewage disposal systems and includes detailed provisions for all aspects of design, installation and inspection of private sewage disposal systems.

International Mechanical Code™. Establishes minimum regulations for mechanical systems using prescriptive and performance-related provisions. It is founded on broad-based principles that make possible the use of new materials and new mechanical designs.

Uniform Zoning Code™. This code is dedicated to intelligent community development and to the benefit of the public welfare by providing a means of promoting uniformity in zoning laws and enforcement.

***Uniform Fire Code™**, Volumes 1 and 2. The premier model fire code in the United States, the *Uniform Fire Code* sets forth provisions necessary for fire prevention and fire protection. Published by the International Fire Code Institute, the *Uniform Fire Code* is endorsed by the Western Fire Chiefs Association, the International Association of Fire Chiefs and ICBO. Volume 1 contains code provisions compatible with the *Uniform Building Code,* and Volume 2 contains standards referenced from the code provisions.

***Urban-Wildland Interface Code™.** Promulgated by IFCI, this code regulates both land use and the built environment in designated urban-wildland interface areas. This newly developed code is the only model code that bases construction requirements on the fire-hazard severity exposed to the structure. Developed under a grant from the Federal Emergency Management Agency, this code is the direct result of hazard mitigation meetings held after devastating wildfires.

Uniform Housing Code™. Provides complete requirements affecting conservation and rehabilitation of housing. Its regulations are compatible with the *Uniform Building Code.*

Uniform Code for the Abatement of Dangerous Buildings™. A code compatible with the *Uniform Building Code* and the *Uniform Housing Code* which provides equitable remedies consistent with other laws for the repair, vacation or demolition of dangerous buildings.

Uniform Sign Code™. Dedicated to the development of better sign regulation, its requirements pertain to all signs and sign construction attached to buildings.

Uniform Administrative Code™. This code covers administrative areas in connection with adoption of the *Uniform Building Code, Uniform Mechanical Code* and related codes. It contains provisions which relate to site preparation, construction, alteration, moving, repair and use and occupancies of buildings or structures and building service equipment, including plumbing, electrical and mechanical regulations. The code is compatible with the administrative provisions of all codes published by the Conference.

Uniform Building Security Code™. This code establishes minimum standards to make dwelling units resistant to unlawful entry. It regulates swinging doors, sliding doors, windows and hardware in connection with dwelling units of apartment houses or one- and two-family dwellings. The code gives consideration to the concerns of police, fire and building officials in establishing requirements for resistance to burglary which are compatible with fire and life safety.

Uniform Code for Building Conservation™. A building conservation guideline presented in code format which will provide a community with the means to preserve its existing buildings while achieving appropriate levels of safety. It is formatted in the same manner as the *Uniform Building Code,* is compatible with other Uniform Codes, and may be adopted as a code or used as a guideline.

Dwelling Construction under the Uniform Building Code™. Designed primarily for use in home building and apprentice training, this book contains requirements applicable to the construction of one- and two-story dwellings based on the requirements of the *Uniform Building Code.* Available in English or Spanish.

Dwelling Construction under the Uniform Mechanical Code™. This publication is for the convenience of the homeowner or contractor interested in installing mechanical equipment in a one- or two-family dwelling in conformance with the *Uniform Mechanical Code.*

Supplements to UBC and related codes. Published in the years between editions, the Supplements contain all approved changes, plus an analysis of those changes.

Uniform Building Code—1927 Edition. A special 60th anniversary printing of the first published *Uniform Building Code.*

One and Two Family Dwelling Code. Promulgated by ICC, this code eliminates conflicts and duplications among the model codes to achieve national uniformity. Covers mechanical and plumbing requirements as well as construction and occupancy.

Application and Commentary on the One and Two Family Dwelling Code. An interpretative commentary on the *One and Two Family Dwelling Code* intended to enhance uniformity of interpretation and application of the code nationwide. Developed by the three model code organizations, this document includes numerous illustrations of code requirements and the rationale for individual provisions.

Model Energy Code. This code includes minimum requirements for effective use of energy in the design of new buildings and structures and additions to existing buildings. It is based on American Society of Heating, Refrigeration and Air-conditioning Engineers Standard 90A-1980 and was originally developed jointly by ICBO, BOCA, SBCCI and the National Conference of States on Building Codes and Standards under a contract funded by the United States Department of Energy. The code is now maintained by ICC and is adopted by reference in the *Uniform Building Code.*

National Electrical Code®. The electrical code used throughout the United States. Published by the National Fire Protection Association, it is an indispensable aid to every electrician, contractor, architect, builder, inspector and anyone who must specify or certify electrical installations.

TECHNICAL REFERENCES AND EDUCATIONAL MATERIALS

Analysis of Revisions to the Uniform Codes™. An analysis of changes between the previous and new editions of the Uniform Codes is provided. Changes between code editions are noted either at the beginning of chapters or in the margins of the code text.

***Handbook to the Uniform Building Code.** The handbook is a completely detailed and illustrated commentary on the *Uniform Building Code,* tracing historical background and rationale of the codes through the current edition. Also included are numerous drawings and figures clarifying the application and intent of the code provisions. Also available in electronic format.

***Handbook to the Uniform Mechanical Code.** An indispensable tool for understanding the provisions of the current UMC, the handbook traces the historical background and rationale behind the UMC provisions, includes 160 figures which clarify the intent and application of the code, and provides a chapter-by-chapter analysis of the UMC.

***Uniform Building Code Application Manual.** This manual discusses sections of the *Uniform Building Code* with a question-and-answer format, providing a comprehensive analysis of the intent of the code sections. Most sections include illustrative examples. The manual is in loose-leaf format so that code applications published in *Building Standards* magazine may be inserted. Also available in electronic format.

***Uniform Mechanical Code Application Manual.** As a companion document to the *Uniform Mechanical Code,* this manual provides a comprehensive analysis of the intent of a number of code sections in an easy-to-use question-and-answer format. The manual is available in a loose-leaf format and includes illustrative examples for many code sections.

***Uniform Fire Code Applications Manual.** This newly developed manual provides questions and answers regarding UFC provisions. A comprehensive analysis of the intent of numerous code sections, the manual is in a loose-leaf format for easy insertion of code applications published in IFCI's *Fire Code Journal.*

Quick-Reference Guide to the Occupancy Requirements of the 1997 UBC. Code requirements are compiled in this publication by occupancy groups for quick access. These tabulations assemble requirements for each occupancy classification in the code. Provisions, such as fire-resistive ratings for occupancy separations in Table 3-B, exterior wall and opening protection requirements in Table 5-A-1, and fire-resistive ratings for types of construction in Table 6-A, are tabulated for quick reference and comparison.

Plan Review Manual. A practical text that will assist and guide both the field inspector and plan reviewer in applying the code requirements. This manual covers the nonstructural and basic structural aspects of plan review.

Field Inspection Manual. An important fundamental text for courses of study at the community college and trade or technical school level. It is an effective text for those studying building construction or architecture and includes sample forms and checklists for use in the field.

Building Department Administration. An excellent guide for improvement of skills in departmental management and in the enforcement and application of the Building Code and other regulations administered by a building inspection department. This textbook will also be a valuable aid to instructors, students and those in related professional fields.

Building Department Guide to Disaster Mitigation. This new, expanded guide is designed to assist building departments in developing or updating disaster mitigation plans. Subjects covered include guidelines for damage mitigation, disaster-response management, immediate response, mutual aid and inspections, working with the media, repair and recovery policies, and public information bulletins. This publication is a must for those involved in preparing for and responding to disaster.

Building Official Management Manual. This manual addresses the unique nature of code administration and the managerial duties of the building official. A supplementary insert addresses the budgetary and financial aspects of a building department. It is also an ideal resource for those preparing for the management module of the CABO Building Official Certification Examination.

Legal Aspects of Code Administration. A manual developed by the three model code organizations to inform the building official on the legal aspects of the profession. The text is written in a logical sequence with explanation of legal terminology. It is designed to serve as a refresher for those preparing to take the legal module of the CABO Building Official Certification Examination.

Illustrated Guide to Conventional Construction Provisions of the UBC. This comprehensive guide and commentary provides detailed explanations of the conventional construction provisions in the UBC, including descriptive discussions and illustrated drawings to convey the prescriptive provisions related to wood-frame construction.

Introduction to the Uniform Building Code. A workbook that provides an overview of the basics of the UBC.

Uniform Building Code Update Workbook. This manual addresses many of the changes to the administrative, fire- and life-safety, and inspection provisions appearing in the UBC.

UMC Workbook. Designed for independent study or use with instructor-led programs based on the *Uniform Mechanical Code,* this comprehensive study guide consists of 16 learning sessions, with the first two sessions reviewing the purpose, scope, definitions and administrative provisions and the remaining 14 sessions progressively exploring the requirements for installing, inspecting and maintaining heating, ventilating, cooling and refrigeration systems.

UBC Field Inspection Workbook. A comprehensive workbook for studying the provisions of the UBC. Divided into 12 sessions, this workbook focuses on the UBC combustible construction requirements for the inspection of wood-framed construction.

Concrete Manual. A publication for individuals seeking an understanding of the fundamentals of concrete field technology and inspection practices. Of particular interest to concrete construction inspectors, it will also benefit employees of concrete producers, contractors, testing and inspection laboratories and material suppliers.

Reinforced Concrete Masonry Construction Inspector's Handbook. A comprehensive information source written especially for masonry inspection covering terminology, technology, materials, quality control, inspection and standards. Published jointly by ICBO and the Masonry Institute of America.

You Can Build It! Sponsored by ICBO in cooperation with CABO, this booklet contains information and advice to aid "do-it-yourselfers" with building projects. Provides guidance in necessary procedures such as permit requirements, codes, plans, cost estimation, etc.

Guidelines for Manufactured Housing Installations. A guideline in code form implementing the *Uniform Building Code* and its companion code documents to regulate the permanent installation of a manufactured home on a privately owned, nonrental site. A commentary is included to explain specific provisions, and codes applying to each component part are defined.

Accessibility Reference Guide. This guide is a valuable resource for architects, interior designers, plan reviewers and others who design and enforce accessibility provisions. Features include accessibility requirements, along with detailed commentary and graphics to clarify the provisions; cross-references to other applicable sections of the UBC and the Americans with Disabilities Act Accessibility Guidelines; a checklist of UBC provisions on access and usability requirements; and many other useful references.

Educational and Technical Reference Materials. The Conference has been a leader in the development of texts and course material to assist in the educational process. These materials include vital information necessary for the building official and subordinates in carrying out their responsibilities and have proven to be excellent references in connection with community college curricula and higher-level courses in the field of building construction technology and inspection and in the administration of building departments. Included are plan review checklists for structural, nonstructural, mechanical and fire-safety provisions and a full line of videotapes and automated products.

TABLE OF CONTENTS

TABLES

FIGURES

LEGAL REQUIREMENTS

(Note: All tables and figures appear at the end of the text.)

Building Permit

A building permit must be obtained from the building official before beginning construction. Permit application forms are furnished by the building official. (Sec. 106)

Investigation fees are charged where work is started before obtaining a permit. (Sec. 107.5)

Information on Plans and Specifications

When applying for a permit, plans and specifications may be required. These plans and specifications must be drawn to scale upon substantial paper or cloth and be of sufficient clarity to indicate the nature and extent of the work proposed and show in detail that it will be in accordance with the Building Code and all relevant laws, ordinances, rules and regulations. Plans must include a plot plan showing the location of the proposed building and of every existing building on the property. A typical plot plan is shown in Figure 1. In lieu of detailed specifications, the building official may approve references on the plans to a specific section or part of the code or other ordinances or laws. (Secs. 106.3.1 and 106.3.3)

Computations, stress diagrams and other data sufficient to show the correctness of the plans shall be submitted when required by the building official. (Sec. 106.3.2)

Inspection Record Card

An inspection record card is assigned to the permit holder when the permit is issued. This card must be posted in a conspicuous place or otherwise made available on the premises and in such position as to allow the building official to conveniently make the required entries thereon regarding inspection of the work. This card must be maintained available by the permit holder until the work is completed and a final inspection has been made. (Sec. 108.2)

Inspections

The permit holder or an agent of the permit holder must notify the building official when the work is ready for inspection. In addition to special inspections which may be necessary, the following inspections are required:

1. **Foundation Inspection.** To be made after excavations for footings are complete and any required reinforcing steel is in place. For concrete foundations, forms shall be in place prior to inspection. All materials for the foundation shall be on the job, except where concrete is ready mixed in accordance with ASTM C 94, the concrete need not be on the job. Where the foundation is to be constructed of approved treated wood, additional inspections may be required by the building official. (Sec. 108.5.2)

2. **Concrete Slab or Under-floor Inspection.** To be made after all in-slab or under-floor building service equipment, conduit, piping accessories and other ancillary equipment items are in place but before any concrete is placed or floor sheathing installed, including the subfloor. (Sec. 108.5.3).

3. **Frame Inspection.** To be made after the roof, all framing, fire-blocking and bracing are in place and all pipes, chimneys and vents are complete and the rough electrical, plumbing and heating wires, pipes and ducts are approved. (Sec. 108.5.4)

4. **Lath and/or Gypsum Board Inspection.** To be made after all lathing and/or gypsum board, interior and exterior, is in place but before any plastering is applied or before gypsum board joints and fasteners are taped and finished. (Sec. 108.5.5)

5. **Final Inspection.** To be made after finish grade and building is completed and ready for occupancy. (Sec. 108.5.6)

Other inspections and a survey of the lot may also be required by the building official to verify compliance of the structure with the provisions of the *Uniform Building Code* and other laws enforced by the code enforcement agency. (Sec. 108.7)

The building official will either approve that portion of the construction as completed or will notify the permit holder or an agent of the permit holder wherein the same fails to comply with the law. (Sec. 108.4)

LOCATION ON THE LOT

Except where zoning regulations are more restrictive, any exterior wall having windows or other openings must be at least 3 feet (914 mm) from the property line. Other walls may be less than 3 feet (914 mm) from property lines but must be of at least one-hour fire-resistive construction. (Sec. 503)

One-hour fire-resistive construction includes the following:

1. Exterior plaster over metal or wire lath on the outside and $^5/_8$-inch (15.9 mm) Type X gypsum wallboard on the inside.

2. Three-fourths-inch (19 mm) drop siding over $^1/_2$-inch (12.7 mm) gypsum sheathing on 2-inch by 4-inch (51 mm by 102 mm) wood studs at 16 inches (406 mm) on center on exterior surface with interior surface treatment as specified in Item 1. Gypsum sheathing nailed with $1^3/_4$-inch (44.5 mm) by No. 11 gage by $^7/_{16}$-inch (11.1 mm) head galvanized nails at 8 inches (203 mm) on center. Siding nailed with 7-penny galvanized smooth box nails.

See Table 7-B of the *Uniform Building Code* for additional assemblies.

SEPARATION BETWEEN DWELLING UNITS

Walls and floors separating dwelling units in the same building shall not be less than one-hour fire-resistive construction. (Sec. 310.2)

LIGHT, VENTILATION AND SANITATION

Windows and Ventilation

Living rooms and other rooms used for living, dining or sleeping purposes (habitable rooms, except for kitchens) shall be provided with natural light by means of exterior glazed openings with an area not less than one tenth of the floor area of such rooms with a minimum of 10 square feet (0.93 m^2). Bathrooms, water closet compartments and similar rooms shall be provided with natural ventilation by means of openable exterior openings with an area not less than one twentieth of the floor area of such rooms with a minimum of $1^1/_2$ square feet (0.14 m^2).

Habitable rooms within a dwelling unit shall be provided with natural ventilation by means of openable exterior openings with an area of not less than one twentieth of the floor area of such rooms with a minimum of 5 square feet (0.46 m^2). (Sec. 1203.3)

In lieu of required exterior openings for natural ventilation, a mechanical ventilation system may be provided. Such system shall be capable of providing two air changes per hour in all habitable rooms with a minimum of 15 cubic feet per minute (7 L/s) of outside air per occupant during such time as the building is occupied. In bathrooms containing a bathtub or shower or combination thereof and similar rooms, a mechanical ventilation system connected directly to the outside capable of providing five air changes per hour shall be provided. The point of discharge of exhaust air shall be at least 3 feet (914 mm) from any opening which allows air entry into occupied portions of the building. Bathrooms which contain only a water closet or lavatory or combination thereof, and similar rooms may be ventilated with an approved mechanical recirculating fan or similar device designed to remove odors from the air.

For the purpose of determining light and ventilation requirements, any room may be considered as a portion of an adjoining room when one half of the area of the common wall is open and unobstructed and provides an opening of not less than one tenth of the floor area of the interior room or 25 square feet (2.3 m^2), whichever is greater.

Exterior openings for natural light and ventilation shall open directly onto a public way or a yard or court located on the same lot as the building. (Sec. 1203.1)

EXCEPTIONS: 1. Required exterior windows may open into a roofed porch where the porch:

1.1 Abuts a public way, yard or court;

1.2 Has a ceiling height of not less than 7 feet (2134 mm); and

1.3 Has the longer side at least 65 percent open and unobstructed.

2. Skylights.

Eaves over required windows shall not be less than 30 inches (762 mm) from the side and rear property lines. (Sec. 1204)

Ceiling Heights

Habitable space shall have a ceiling height of not less than 7 feet 6 inches (2286 mm) except as otherwise permitted in this section. Kitchens, halls, bathrooms and toilet compartments may have a ceiling height of not less than 7 feet (2134 mm) measured to the lowest projection from the ceiling. Where exposed beam ceiling members are spaced at less than 48 inches (1219 mm) on center, ceiling height shall be measured to the bottom of these members. Where exposed beam ceiling members are spaced at 48 inches (1219 mm) or more on center, ceiling height shall be measured to the bottom of the deck supported by these members, provided that the bottom of the members is not less than 7 feet (2134 mm) above the floor.

If any room in a building has a sloping ceiling, the prescribed ceiling height for the room is required in only one-half the area thereof. No portion of the room measuring less than 5 feet (1524 mm) from the finished floor to the finished ceiling shall be included in any computation of the minimum area thereof.

If any room has a furred ceiling, the prescribed ceiling height is required in two-thirds the area thereof, but in no case shall the height of the furred ceiling be less than 7 feet (2134 mm). (Sec. 310.6.1)

Sanitation

Sanitation facilities shall be provided as required by the local ordinances.

A room in which a water closet is located shall be separated from food preparation or storage rooms by a tightfitting door. (Sec. 302.6)

Every dwelling unit shall be provided with a kitchen equipped with a kitchen sink. Every dwelling unit and every lodging house shall be provided with a bathroom equipped with facilities consisting of a water closet, lavatory and either a bathtub or shower. Each sink, lavatory and either a bathtub or shower shall be equipped with hot and cold running water necessary for its normal operation. (Sec. 2902.6)

ROOM DIMENSIONS

Dwelling units shall have at least one room which shall not have less than 120 square feet (11.2 m^2) of floor area. Other habitable rooms except kitchens shall have an area of not less than 70 square feet (6.5 m^2). (Sec. 310.6.2)

Habitable rooms other than a kitchen shall not be less than 7 feet (2134 mm) in any dimension. (Sec. 310.6.3)

Each water closet stool shall be located in a clear space not less than 30 inches (762 mm) in width and have a clear space in front of the water closet stool not less than 24 inches (610 mm). (Sec. 2904)

FIRE-WARNING SYSTEM

Dwelling units shall be provided with approved smoke detectors. A detector shall be installed in each sleeping room and at a point centrally located in the corridor or area giving access to each separate sleeping area. When the dwelling unit has more than one story and in dwellings with basements, a detector shall be installed on each story and in the basement. In dwelling units where a story or basement is split into two or more levels, the smoke detector shall be installed on the upper level, except that when the lower level contains a sleeping area, a detector shall be installed on each level. When sleeping rooms are on an upper level, the detector shall be placed at the ceiling of the upper level in close proximity to the stairway.

In dwelling units where the ceiling height of a room open to the hallway serving the bedrooms exceeds that of the hallway by 24 inches (610 mm) or more, smoke detectors shall be installed in the hallway and in the adjacent room.

Detectors shall be installed in accordance with approved manufacturer's instructions. When actuated, the detector shall provide an alarm that is audible within sleeping areas. (Sec. 310.9.1.4)

When the valuation of an addition, alteration or repair exceeds $1,000.00 and a permit is required, or when one or more sleeping rooms are added or created in existing dwellings, the entire building shall be provided with smoke detectors located as required for new dwellings. This requirement is not applicable for repairs made to the exterior surfaces of the dwelling. (Sec. 310.9.1.2)

In new construction, required smoke detectors shall receive their primary power from the building wiring when such wiring is served from a commercial source and shall be equipped with a battery backup. The detector shall emit a signal when the batteries are low. Wiring shall be permanent and without a disconnecting switch other than those required for overcurrent protection. Smoke detectors may be solely battery operated when installed in existing buildings, or in buildings without commercial power, or in buildings which undergo alterations, repairs or additions regulated by the previous paragraph. (Sec. 310.9.1.3)

EXITS

Doors

At least one doorway from dwellings shall be of a size as to permit the installation of a door not less than 3 feet (914 mm) in width and not less than 6 feet 8 inches (2032 mm) in height. The door shall be so mounted that the clear width of the exitway is not less than 32 inches (813 mm). (Sec. 1003.3.1)

Door Landings

There shall be a floor or landing on each side of all doors. The floor or landing shall be level, except for exterior landings which may have a slope not to exceed $^1/_4$ unit vertical in 12 units horizontal (2% slope), with the floor or landing not more than 1 inch (25 mm) lower than the threshold of the doorway. However, in private dwellings a door may open at the top step of an interior flight of stairs or at a landing, provided the door does not swing over that top step or landing (except that screen doors and storm doors may) and the landing is not more than 8 inches (203 mm) below the floor level. The landing shall have a width not less than the width of the stairway or the width of the door, whichever is the greater. The landing shall have a length measured in the direction of travel of not less than 36 inches (914 mm). (Secs. 1003.3.1.6 and 1003.3.1.7)

EMERGENCY ESCAPE OR RESCUE WINDOWS

Basements in dwelling units and every sleeping room below the fourth story shall have at least one operable window or exterior door approved for emergency escape or rescue which opens directly into a public street, public alley, yard or exit court. The units shall be operable from the inside to provide a full clear opening without the use of separate tools.

All escape or rescue windows from sleeping rooms shall have a minimum net clear openable area of 5.7 square feet (0.53 m^2). The minimum net clear openable height dimension shall be 24 inches (610 mm). The minimum net clear openable width dimension shall be 20 inches (508 mm). When windows are provided as a means of escape or rescue they shall have a finished sill height not more than 44 inches (1118 mm) above the floor.

Escape and rescue windows with a finished sill height below the adjacent ground elevation shall have a window well. Window wells at escape or rescue windows shall comply with the following:

1. The clear horizontal dimensions shall allow the window to be fully opened and provide a minimum accessible net clear opening of 9 square feet (0.84 m^2), with a minimum dimension of 36 inches (914 mm).

2. Window wells with a vertical depth of more than 44 inches (1118 mm) shall be equipped with an approved, permanently affixed ladder or stairs that are accessible with the window in the fully open position. The ladder or stairs shall not encroach into the required dimensions of the window well by more than 6 inches (152 mm). (Sec. 310.4)

Bars, grilles, grates or similar devices may be installed on an emergency escape or on rescue windows, doors or window wells, provided:

1. The devices are equipped with approved release mechanisms which are openable from the inside without the use of a key or special knowledge or effort, and

2. The building is equipped with smoke detectors installed in accordance with Section 310.9 of the *Uniform Building Code.*

STAIRS

Rise and Run (See Figure 2.)

The rise of steps in a stairway shall not be less than 4 inches (102 mm) or greater than 7 inches (178 mm) and the run shall not be less than 11 inches (279 mm). The largest tread run within any flight of stairs shall not exceed the smallest by more than $^3/_8$ inch (9.5 mm). The greatest riser height within any flight of stairs shall not exceed the smallest by more than $^3/_8$ inch (9.5 mm). (Sec. 1003.3.3.3)

EXCEPTIONS: 1. Private stairways serving an occupant load of less than 10 may be constructed with an 8-inch (203 mm) maximum rise and 9-inch (229 mm) minimum run.

2. Where the bottom or top riser adjoins a sloping public way, walk or driveway having an established grade and serving as a landing, the

bottom or top riser may be reduced along the slope to less than 4 inches (102 mm) in height with the variation in height of the bottom or top riser not to exceed 1 unit vertical in 12 units horizontal (8.3% slope) of stairway width.

Winders

In residences, winders may be used if the required width of run is provided at a point not more than 12 inches (305 mm) from the side of the stairway where the treads are narrower, but in no case shall any width of run be less than 6 inches (152 mm) at any point. (Sec. 1003.3.3.8.2)

Spiral Stairs

Spiral stairs may be used for exits when the area served is limited to 400 square feet (37.16 m^2).

For spiral stairways, the tread must provide a clear walking area measuring at least 26 inches (660 mm) from the outer edge of the supporting column to the inner edge of the handrail. A run of at least 7$^1/_2$ inches (191 mm) is to be provided at a point 12 inches (305 mm) from where the tread is the narrowest. The rise or height of the steps shall not exceed 9$^1/_2$ inches (241 mm). (Sec. 1003.3.3.8.3)

Handrails

Stairways shall have at least one handrail, and handrails shall be installed on open sides of stairways.

The top of handrails shall be placed not less than 34 inches (864 mm) or more than 38 inches (965 mm) above the nosing of treads. They shall be continuous the full length of the stair. Ends shall be returned or shall terminate in newel posts or safety terminals.

Handrails projecting from a wall shall have a space of not less than 1$^1/_2$ inches (38 mm) between the wall and the handrail.

The handgrip portion of handrails shall not be less than 1$^1/_4$ inches (32 mm) or more than 2 inches (51 mm) in cross-sectional dimension or the shape shall provide an equivalent gripping surface. The handgrip portion shall have a smooth surface with no sharp corners. (Sec. 1003.3.3.6)

Headroom

Every required stairway shall have headroom clearance of not less than 6 feet 8 inches (2032 mm) measured vertically from the tread nosings to the nearest soffit above. (Sec. 1003.3.3.4)

Guardrails

All unenclosed floor and roof openings, open and glazed sides of landings and ramps, balconies or porches which are more than 30 inches (762 mm) above grade, or the floor below, and roofs used for other than service of building shall be protected by a guardrail. Guardrails shall not be less than 36 inches (914 mm) in height, except on stairways where they may be 34 inches (864 mm). Open guardrails and stair railings shall have intermediate rails or an ornamental pattern such that a sphere 4 inches (102 mm) in diameter cannot pass through. (Sec. 509)

PRIVATE GARAGES AND CARPORTS

A private garage not over 1,000 square feet (99 m^2) in area may be attached to a dwelling if the garage side of the separating walls and ceilings is fire protected as shown in Figure 3. (Sec. 302.4)

A carport having no enclosed uses above and entirely open on two or more sides need not have a fire separation between the carport and the dwelling. (Sec. 302.1)

FOUNDATIONS, RETAINING WALLS AND DRAINAGE

Foundations

Exterior walls and interior bearing walls shall be supported on masonry, concrete or treated-wood footings and foundations which are of sufficient size to safely support the loads imposed as determined from the character of the soil and shall extend below the frost line. Foundation walls shall extend at least 6 inches (152 mm) above the finished grade adjacent to the wall at all points.

Wood plates or sills shall be bolted to the foundation or foundation wall. Steel bolts with a minimum nominal diameter of $^1/_2$ inch (12.7 mm) shall be used in Seismic Zones 0 through 3. Steel bolts with a minimum nominal diameter of $^5/_8$ inch (16 mm) shall be used in Seismic Zone 4. Bolts shall be embedded at least 7 inches (178 mm) into the concrete or masonry and shall be spaced not more than 6 feet (1829 mm) apart. There shall be a minimum of two bolts per piece with one bolt located not more than 12 inches (305 mm) or less than seven bolt diameters from each end of the piece. A properly sized nut and washer shall be tightened on each bolt to the plate. Foundation plates and sills shall be the kind of wood specified in Section 2306.4.

The following additional requirements shall apply in Seismic Zones 3 and 4.

1. Sill bolt diameter and spacing for three-story raised wood floor buildings shall be specifically designed.

2. Plate washers a minimum of 2 inch by 2 inch by $^3/_{16}$ inch (51 mm by 51 mm by 4.8 mm) thick shall be used on each bolt.

In Seismic Zones 3 and 4, horizontal reinforcement in accordance with Sections 1806.7.1 and 1806.7.2 shall be placed in continuous foundations to minimize differential settlement. Foundation reinforcement shall be provided with cover in accordance with Section 1907.7.1.

Foundations with stemwalls shall be provided with a minimum of one No. 4 bar at the top of the wall and one No. 4 bar at the bottom of the footing.

Slabs-on-ground with turned-down footings shall have a minimum of one No. 4 bar at the top and bottom.

EXCEPTION: For slabs-on-ground cast monolithically with a footing, one No. 5 bar may be located at either the top or bottom.

See Figure 4. (Secs. 1806.1 and 1806.6 and Table 18-I-C)

When expansive soils are present, the building official may require that special provisions be made in the foundation design and construction to safeguard against damage due to this expansiveness. The building official may require a special investigation and report to provide this design and construction criteria. (Sec. 1804.4)

Foundation plates or sills shall be of wood pressure treated with an approved preservative, or Foundation grade redwood, all marked or branded by an approved agency. (Sec. 2306.4)

Foundations for all buildings where the surface of the ground slopes more than 1 unit vertical in 10 units horizontal (10% slope) shall be level or shall be stepped so that both top and bottom of such foundation are level. (Sec. 1806.4)

Dampproofing Foundation Walls

Unless otherwise approved by the building official, foundation walls enclosing a basement below finished grade shall be dampproofed outside by approved methods and materials. (Sec. 1402.4)

Retaining Walls

Walls retaining earth are required to be designed for the loads specified in Section 1611.6 of the *Uniform Building Code.*

Drainage

Provisions shall be made for the control and drainage of surface water around buildings. (Secs. 1804.7 and 1806.5.5)

CHIMNEYS, FIREPLACES AND BARBECUES

For details of chimney, fireplace and barbecue construction, see Figure 5. The following requirements and Figure 5 are for brick construction; for other materials, the builder should consult the *Uniform Building Code.*

Reinforcing and Seismic Anchorage

Unless a specific design is provided, every masonry or concrete chimney in Seismic Zones 2, 3 and 4 shall be reinforced with not less than four No. 4 steel reinforcing bars conforming to the provisions of Chapter 19 or 21 of the *Uniform Building Code*. The bars shall extend the full height of the chimney and shall be spliced in accordance with the applicable requirements of Chapters 19 and 21. In masonry chimneys, the vertical bars shall have a minimum cover of $^{1}/_{2}$ inch (12.7 mm) of grout or mortar tempered to a pouring consistency. The bars shall be tied horizontally at 18-inch (457 mm) intervals with not less than $^{1}/_{4}$-inch-diameter (6.4 mm) steel ties. The slope of the inclined portion of the offset in vertical bars shall not exceed 2 units vertical in 1 unit horizontal (200% slope). Two ties shall also be placed at each bend in vertical bars. Where the width of the chimney exceeds 40 inches (1016 mm), two additional No. 4 vertical bars shall be provided for each additional flue incorporated in the chimney or for each additional 40 inches (1016 mm) in width or fraction thereof.

In Seismic Zones 2, 3 and 4, all masonry and concrete chimneys shall be anchored at each floor or ceiling line more than 6 feet (1829 mm) above grade, except when constructed completely within the exterior walls of the building. Anchorage shall consist of two $^{3}/_{16}$-inch by 1-inch (4.8 mm by 25 mm) steel straps cast at least 12 inches (305 mm) into the chimney with a 180-degree bend with a 6-inch (152 mm) extension around the vertical reinforcing bars in the outer face of the chimney.

Each strap shall be fastened to the structural framework of the building with two $^{1}/_{2}$-inch-diameter (12.7 mm) bolts per strap. Where the joists do not head into the chimney, the anchor straps shall be connected to 2-inch by 4-inch (51 mm by 102 mm) ties crossing a minimum of four joists. The ties shall be connected to each joist with two 16d nails. As an alternative to the 2-inch by 4-inch (51 mm by 102 mm) ties, each anchor strap shall be connected to the structural framework by two $^{1}/_{2}$-inch-diameter (12.7 mm) bolts in an approved manner. (Sec. 3102.4.3)

Metal chimneys shall be anchored at each floor and roof with two $1^{1}/_{2}$-inch by $^{1}/_{8}$-inch (38 mm by 3.2 mm) metal straps looped around the outside of the chimney installations and nailed with six 8d nails per strap to the roof or ceiling framing. (Sec. 3102.6)

Flue Area

The minimum net cross-sectional area of the chimney flue for fireplaces shall be determined in accordance with Figure 31-1 of the *Uniform Building Code.* The minimum cross-sectional area shown or a flue size providing equivalent net cross-sectional area shall be used. The height of the chimney shall be measured from the firebox floor to the top of the last chimney flue tile. Chimney passageways for low-heat chimneys and incinerators shall not be smaller in area than the vent connection on the appliance attached thereto or not less than that set forth in Table 31-A. (Secs. 3102.3.5 and 3102.7.9)

EXCEPTION: Chimney passageways designed by engineering methods approved by the building official.

The throat shall be at least 8 inches (203 mm) above the fireplace opening. The throat shall be at least 4 inches (102 mm) in depth. The net cross-sectional area of the flue and of the throat between the firebox and the smoke chamber of a fireplace shall not be less than that set forth in Figure 31-1 or Table 31-A. Metal dampers equivalent to not less than 0.097 inch (2.46 mm) (No. 12 carbon sheet metal gage) steel shall be installed. When fully open, damper openings shall not be less than 90 percent of the required flue area.

Height

Every chimney shall extend at least 2 feet (610 mm) above the part of the roof through which it passes and at least 2 feet (610 mm) above the highest elevation of any portion of the building within 10 feet (3048 mm) of the chimney. For altitudes over 2,000 feet (610 m), the building official shall be consulted in determining the height of the chimney. (Sec. 3102.3.6)

Inlets

Every inlet to any masonry chimney shall enter the side thereof and shall be of not less than $^{1}/_{8}$-inch-thick (3.2 mm) metal or $^{5}/_{8}$-inch-thick (16 mm) refractory material. Where there is no other opening below the inlet other than the cleanout, a masonry plug shall be constructed in the chimney not more than 16 inches (406 mm) below the inlet and the cleanout shall be located where it is accessible above the plug. If the plug is located less than 6 inches (152 mm) below the inlet, the inlet may serve as the cleanout. (Sec. 3102.4.7)

Loads on Chimney

A chimney shall not support any structural load other than its own weight unless it is designed to act as a supporting member. (Sec. 3102.3.1)

MASONRY FIREPLACES

Fireplace Walls

Masonry walls of fireplaces shall not be less than 8 inches (203 mm) in thickness. Walls of fireboxes shall not be less than 10 inches (254 mm) in thickness, except that where a lining of firebrick is used, such walls shall not be less than 8 inches (203 mm) in thickness. The firebox shall not be less than 20 inches (508 mm) in depth. The maximum thickness of joints in firebrick shall be $^{1}/_{4}$ inch (6 mm). An exception is made for Rumford fireplaces where the depth may be reduced to 12 inches (305 mm) when:

1. The depth is at least one third of the width of the fireplace opening.

2. The throat is at least 12 inches (305 mm) above the lintel and is at least one twentieth of the cross-sectional area of the fireplace opening. (Sec. 3102.7.3)

Approved metal heat circulators may be installed in fireplaces. (Sec. 3102.7.5)

Lintel

Masonry over the fireplace opening shall be supported by a noncombustible lintel unless the masonry is self-supporting. (Sec. 3102.7.10)

Hearth

Masonry fireplaces shall be provided with a brick, concrete, stone or other approved noncombustible hearth slab. This slab shall not be less than 4 inches (102 mm) thick and shall be supported by noncombustible materials or reinforced to carry its own weight and all imposed loads. Combustible forms and centering shall be removed. (Sec. 3102.7.11)

Hearth Extensions

Hearths shall extend at least 16 inches (406 mm) from the front of, and at least 8 inches (203 mm) beyond each side of, the fireplace opening. Where the fireplace opening is 6 square feet (0.56 m^2) or larger, the hearth extension shall extend at least 20 inches (508 mm) in front of, and at least 12 inches (305 mm) beyond each side of, the fireplace opening.

Except for fireplaces which open to the exterior of the building, hearth slabs shall be readily distinguishable from the surrounding or adjacent floor. (Sec. 3102.7.12)

Combustible Materials

Combustible materials shall not be placed within 6 inches (152 mm) of the fireplace opening. Combustible material within 12 inches (305 mm) of the fireplace opening shall not project more than $^{1}/_{8}$ inch (3 mm) for each 1-inch (25 mm) clearance from such opening. (Sec. 3102.7.8)

Support

Masonry fireplaces shall be supported on foundations designed as required in Chapters 16, 18 and 21 of the *Uniform Building Code.* (Sec. 3102.7.2)

MASONRY CHIMNEYS

Lining

Where lining is required, chimneys shall be lined with clay flue tile, firebrick, molded refractory units or other approved lining not less than $^{5}/_{8}$ inch (15.9 mm) thick. Chimney liners shall be carefully bedded in approved medium-duty refractory mortar with close-fitting joints left smooth on the inside. Medium-duty refractory mortar shall be in accordance with Sections 3503 and 3504 and ASTM C 199. (Sec. 3102.3.4 and Table 31-B)

Wall Thickness

Masonry chimneys shall be constructed of masonry units or reinforced concrete with walls not less than 4 inches (102 mm) thick when lined or 8 inches (203 mm) thick when unlined or rubble stone masonry not less than 12 inches (305 mm) thick. (Table 31-B)

Clearance

Combustible materials shall not be placed within 2 inches (51 mm) of fireplaces, smoke chambers or chimneys. For special conditions covering fireplaces, see below. (Sec. 3102.7.8)

FACTORY-BUILT CHIMNEYS

Factory-built chimneys shall be installed in strict accordance with their listings and the manufacturer's instructions as specified in the Mechanical Code. (Sec. 3102.5)

FRAMING—GENERAL

Workmanship

All members shall be framed, anchored, tied and braced so as to develop the strength and rigidity necessary for the purposes for which they are to be used. For details of framing, see Figure 6. (Sec. 2304.4.1)

Spacing and Penetration of Nails

All spacing and edge and end distances shall be such as to avoid splitting of the wood. Holes for nails, when necessary to prevent splitting, shall be bored of a diameter smaller than that of the nails. (Sec. 2318.3)

Tables 23-II-B-1 and 23-II-B-2 comply with the *Uniform Building Code* for number of nails for connecting wood members.

Columns or Posts

Columns and posts located on concrete or masonry floors or decks exposed to the weather or to water splash or in basements, and which support permanent structures, shall be supported by concrete piers or metal pedestals projecting above floors unless approved wood of natural resistance to decay or treated wood is used. The pedestals shall project at least 6 inches (152 mm) above exposed earth and at least 1 inch (25 mm) above such floors.

Individual concrete or masonry piers shall project at least 8 inches (203 mm) above exposed ground unless the columns or posts which they support are of approved wood of natural resistance to decay, or treated wood is used. (Sec. 2306.5)

Wood and Earth Separation

Wood used in construction of permanent structures and located nearer than 6 inches (152 mm) to earth shall be treated wood or wood of natural resistance to decay. Where located on concrete slabs placed on earth, wood shall be treated wood or wood of natural resistance to decay. Where not subject to water splash or to exterior moisture and located on concrete having a minimum thickness of 3 inches (76 mm) with an impervious membrane installed between concrete and earth, the wood may be of any species.

Where planter boxes are installed adjacent to wood frame walls, a 2-inch-wide (51 mm) air space shall be provided between the planter and the wall. Flashings shall be installed when the air space is less than 6 inches (152 mm) in width. Where flashing is used, provisions shall be made to permit circulation of air in the air space. The wood frame wall shall be provided with an exterior wall covering. (Sec. 2306.8)

Headers

Headers and lintels shall be properly designed to support dead loads and design live loads. See Figure 7 for typical framing details. (Sec. 2320.11.6)

FLOOR CONSTRUCTION

Floors shall be constructed as shown in Figure 8.

The allowable spans for floor joists of a grade shall be as set forth in Tables 23-IV-J-1 and 23-IV-J-2 of the *Uniform Building Code*. (Sec. 2320.8) Allowable spans for various grades of wood floor sheathing are shown in Tables 23-II-D-1, 23-II-E-1, 23-II-F-1 and 23-II-F-2 of the *Uniform Building Code*.

Foundation Ventilation and Underfloor Clearance

Underfloor areas shall be ventilated by an approved mechanical means or by openings into the underfloor area walls. Such openings shall have a net area of not less than 1 square foot for each 150 square feet (0.067 m^2 for each 10 m^2) of underfloor area. Openings shall be located as close to corners as practical and shall provide cross ventilation. The required area of such openings shall be approximately equally distributed along the length of at least two opposite sides. They shall be covered with corrosion-resistant wire mesh with mesh openings of $^1/_4$ inch (6.4 mm) in dimension. Where moisture due to climate and groundwater conditions is not considered excessive, the building official may allow operable louvers and may allow the required net area of vent openings to be reduced to 10 percent of the above, provided the underfloor ground surface area is covered with an approved vapor retarder. (Sec. 2306.7)

Minimum clearance between bottom of floor joist or bottom of floors without joists and the ground beneath shall be 18 inches (457 mm). Minimum clearance under girders shall be 12 inches (305 mm). (Sec. 2306.3)

ROOF FRAMING

Design

Where the roof is not designed as specified in Chapter 23 of the *Uniform Building Code*, Tables 23-IV-R-1 through 23-IV-R-12 give the maximum allowable spans for roof rafters. For ceiling joists, see Tables 23-IV-J-3 and 23-IV-J-4. In areas subject to snowfall, verification shall be obtained from the building official as to the design snow load or the appropriate rafter table to use.

The allowable span of roof rafters shall be measured along the horizontal projection between supports.

Roof framing and trusses shall be supported laterally to prevent rotation and lateral displacement. Roof joists when supported on a ribbon board shall be well nailed to the stud. Roof framing detail is illustrated in Figure 9.

Allowable spans in various grades of wood roof sheathing are shown in Tables 23-II-D-1 and 23-II-E-2.

WALL CONSTRUCTION—WOOD

Wall and Partition Framing

1. **Size, height and spacing.** The size, height and spacing of studs shall be in accordance with Table 23-IV-B except that Utility grade studs shall not be spaced more than 16 inches (406 mm) on center, nor support more than a roof and ceiling, nor exceed 8 feet (2438 mm) in height for exterior walls and load-bearing walls or 10 feet (3048 mm) for interior nonload-bearing walls.

2. **Framing details.** Studs shall be placed with their wide dimension perpendicular to the wall. Not less than three studs shall be installed at each corner of an exterior wall.

EXCEPTION: At corners a third stud may be omitted through the use of wood spacers or backup cleats of $^3/_8$-inch-thick (9.5 mm) wood structural panel, $^3/_8$-inch (9.5 mm) Type 2-M particleboard, 1-inch-thick (25 mm) lumber or other approved devices which will serve as an adequate backing for the attachment of facing materials. Where fire-resistance ratings or shear values are involved, wood spacers, backup cleats or other devices shall not be used unless specifically approved for such use.

Bearing and exterior wall studs shall be capped with double top plates installed to provide overlapping at corners and at intersections with other partitions. End joints in double top plates shall be offset at least 48 inches (1219 mm).

EXCEPTION: A single top plate may be used, provided the plate is adequately tied at joints, corners and intersecting walls by at least the equivalent of 3-inch by 6-inch by 0.036-inch-thick (76 mm by 152 mm by 0.9 mm) galvanized steel that is nailed to each wall or segment of wall by six 8d nails or equivalent, provided the rafters, joists or trusses are centered over the studs with a tolerance of no more than 1 inch (25 mm).

When bearing studs are spaced at 24-inch (610 mm) intervals and top plates are less than two 2-inch by 6-inch (51 mm by 152 mm) or two 3-inch by 4-inch (76 mm by 102 mm) members and when the floor joists, floor trusses or roof trusses which they support are spaced at more then 16-inch (406 mm) intervals, such joists or trusses shall bear within 5 inches (127 mm) of the studs beneath or a third plate shall be installed.

Interior nonbearing partitions may be capped with a single top plate installed to provide overlapping at corners and at intersections with other walls and partitions. The plate shall be continuously tied at joints by solid blocking at least 16 inches (406 mm) in length and equal in size to the plate or by $^1/_8$-inch-by-1$^1/_2$-inch (3.2 mm by 38 mm) metal ties with spliced sections fastened with two 16d nails on each side of the joint.

Studs shall have full bearing on a plate or sill not less than 2 inches (51 mm) in thickness having a width not less than that of the wall studs. Wall framing detail is shown in Figure 7. (Sec. 2320.11)

Bracing

In Seismic Zones 0, 1, 2 and 3, where the basic wind speed is not greater than 80 miles per hour (mph) (129 km/h), dwellings shall be provided with exterior and interior braced wall lines. Spacing shall not exceed 34 feet (10 363 mm) on center in both the longitudinal and transverse directions in each story.

In Seismic Zone 4, dwellings shall be provided with exterior and interior braced wall lines. Spacing shall not exceed 25 feet (7620 mm) on center in both the longitudinal and transverse directions in each story.

EXCEPTION: In one- and two-story dwellings, interior braced wall line spacing may be increased to not more than 34 feet (10 363 mm) on center in order to accommodate one single room per dwelling not exceeding 900 square feet (83.61 m^2). The building official may require additional walls to contain braced panels when this exception is used.

See Section 2320 in the *Uniform Building Code* for additional special requirements specific to the seismic zone.

Wall bracing is required in accordance with Table 23-IV-C-1. (Sec. 2320.11)

Braced wall lines shall consist of braced wall panels which meet the requirements for location, type and amount of bracing specified in Table 23-IV-C-1 and are in line or offset from each other by not more than 4 feet (1219 mm). Braced wall panels shall start at not more than 8 feet (2438 mm) from each end of a braced wall line. All braced wall panels shall be clearly indicated on the plans. Construction of braced wall panels shall be by one of the following methods:

1. Nominal 1-inch by 4-inch (25 mm by 102 mm) continuous diagonal braces let into top and bottom plates and intervening studs, placed at an angle not more than 60 degrees or less than 45 degrees from the horizontal, and attached to the framing in conformance with Table 23-II-B-1.

2. Wood boards of $^5/_8$-inch (16 mm) net minimum thickness applied diagonally on studs spaced not over 24 inches (610 mm) on center.

3. Wood structural panel sheathing with a thickness not less than $^5/_{16}$ inch (7.9 mm) for 16-inch (406 mm) stud spacing and not less than $^3/_8$ inch (9.5 mm) for 24-inch (610 mm) stud spacing in accordance with Tables 23-II-A-1 and 23-IV-D-1.

4. Fiberboard sheathing 4-foot by 8-foot (1219 mm by 2438 mm) panels not less than $^1/_2$ inch (13 mm) thick applied vertically on studs spaced not over 16 inches (406 mm) on center when installed in accordance with Section 2315.6 and Table 23-II-J.

5. Gypsum board [sheathing $^1/_2$ inch (13 mm) thick by 4 feet (1219 mm) wide, wallboard or veneer base] on studs spaced not over 24 inches (610 mm) on center and nailed at 7 inches (178 mm) on center with nails as required by Table 25-I.

6. Particleboard wall sheathing panels where installed in accordance with Table 23-IV-D-2.

7. Portland cement plaster on studs spaced 16 inches (406 mm) on center installed in accordance with Table 25-I.

8. Hardboard panel siding when installed in accordance with Section 2310.6 and Table 23-II-C.

Method 1 is not permitted in Seismic Zones 2B, 3 and 4. For cripple wall bracing, see Section 2320.11.5.

For Methods 2, 3, 4, 6, 7 and 8, each braced wall panel must be at least 48 inches (1219 mm) in length, covering three stud spaces where studs are 16 inches (406 mm) apart and covering two stud spaces where studs are spaced 24 inches (610 mm) apart.

For Method 5, each braced wall panel must be at least 96 inches (2438 mm) in length when applied to one face of a braced wall panel and 48 inches (1219 mm) when applied to both faces.

All vertical joints of panel sheathing shall occur over studs. Horizontal joints shall occur over blocking equal in size to the studding except where waived by the installation requirements for the specific sheathing materials.

Braced wall panel sole plates shall be nailed to the floor framing and top plates shall be connected to the framing above in accordance with Table 23-II-B-1. Sills shall be bolted to the foundation or slab in accordance with Section 1806.6. Where joists are perpendicular to braced wall lines above, blocking shall be provided under and in line with the braced wall panels.

Alternate braced wall panels. Any braced wall panel required by Section 2320.11.3 may be replaced by an alternate braced wall panel constructed in accordance with the following:

1. In one-story buildings, each panel shall have a length of not less than 2 feet 8 inches (813 mm) and a height of not more than 10 feet (3048 mm). Each panel shall be sheathed on one face with $^3/_8$-inch-minimum-thickness (9.5 mm) plywood sheathing nailed with 8d common or galvanized box nails in accordance with Table 23-II-B-1 and blocked at all plywood edges. Two anchor bolts installed in accordance with Section 1806.6, shall be provided in each panel. Anchor bolts shall be placed at panel quarter points. Each panel end stud shall have a tie-down device fastened to the foundation, capable of providing an approved uplift capacity of not less than 1,800 pounds (816.5 kg). The tie-down device shall be installed in accordance with the manufacturer's recommendations. The panels shall be supported directly on a foundation or on floor framing supported directly on a foundation which is continuous across the entire length of the braced wall line. This founda-

tion shall be reinforced with not less than one No. 4 bar top and bottom.

2. In the first story of two-story buildings, each braced wall panel shall be in accordance with Section 2320.11.4, Item 1, except that the plywood sheathing shall be provided on both faces, three anchor bolts shall be placed at one-fifth points, and tie-down device uplift capacity shall not be less than 3,000 pounds (1360.8 kg).

Foundation Cripple Studs

Foundation cripple studs shall not be less in size than the studding above and, when exceeding 4 feet (1219 mm) in height, shall be the size required for an additional story. Foundation studs of bearing walls and partitions shall be thoroughly and effectively braced. Cripple walls having a stud height exceeding 14 inches (356 mm) shall be braced in accordance with Table 23-IV-C-2. Solid blocking or wood structural panel sheathing may be used to brace cripple walls having a stud height of 14 inches (356 mm) or less. In Seismic Zone 4, Method 7 is not permitted for bracing any cripple wall studs. (Sec. 2320.11.5)

Fireblocking and Draft Stops

Fireblocking and draftstopping shall be installed to cut off all concealed draft openings (both vertical and horizontal) and shall form an effective barrier between floors, between a top story and a roof or attic space, and shall subdivide attic spaces, concealed roof spaces and floor-ceiling assemblies.

Fireblocking shall be provided in the following locations:

1. In concealed spaces of stud walls and partitions, including furred spaces, at the ceiling and floor levels and at 10-foot (3048 mm) intervals both vertical and horizontal.

> **EXCEPTION:** Fire blocks may be omitted at floor and ceiling levels when approved smoke-actuated fire dampers are installed at these levels.

2. At all interconnections between concealed vertical and horizontal spaces such as occur at soffits, drop ceilings and cove ceilings.

3. In concealed spaces between stair stringers at the top and bottom of the run and between studs along and in line with the run of stairs, if the walls under the stairs are unfinished.

4. In openings around vents, pipes, ducts, chimneys, fireplaces and similar openings which afford a passage for fire at ceiling and floor levels, with noncombustible materials.

5. At openings between attic spaces and chimney chases for factory-built chimneys.

Except as provided in Item 4, fireblocking shall consist of 2 inches (51 mm) nominal lumber or two thicknesses of 1-inch (25 mm) nominal lumber with broken lap joints or one thickness of $^{23}/_{32}$-inch (18.3 mm) wood structural panel with joints backed by $^{23}/_{32}$-inch (18.3 mm) wood structural panel or one thickness of $^{3}/_{4}$-inch (19.1 mm) Type 2-M particleboard with joints backed by $^{3}/_{4}$-inch (19.1 mm) Type 2-M particleboard.

Fire blocks may also be of gypsum board, cement asbestos board, mineral fiber, glass fiber or other approved materials securely fastened in place. Loose-fill insulation material shall not be used as a fire block unless specifically fire tested. (Sec. 708.2)

Draftstopping shall be provided when there is usable space above and below the concealed space of a floor-ceiling assembly so that the area of the concealed space does not exceed 1,000 square feet (93 m^2). Draftstopping shall divide the concealed space into approximately equal areas.

Draftstopping materials shall not be less than $^{1}/_{2}$-inch (12.7 mm) gypsum board, $^{3}/_{8}$-inch (9.5 mm) wood structural panel, $^{3}/_{8}$-inch (9.5 mm) Type 2-M particleboard or other approved materials adequately supported.

Openings in the partitions shall be protected by self-closing doors with automatic latches constructed as required for the partitions. (Sec. 708.3)

WEATHER PROTECTION

Weather-resistive Barriers on Studs

An approved water-resistant paper shall be applied over studs or sheathing of all exterior walls. (Sec. 1402.1)

Water-resistant paper may be omitted in the following cases:

1. When exterior covering is of approved weatherproof panels.
2. In back-plastered construction.
3. When there is no human occupancy.
4. Over water-repellent panel sheathing.
5. Under approved paperbacked metal or wire fabric lath.
6. Behind lath and portland cement plaster applied to the underside of roof and eave projections.

Waterproofing Weather-exposed Horizontal Surfaces

Balconies, landings, exterior stairways, occupied roofs and similar surfaces exposed to the weather and sealed underneath shall be waterproofed and sloped a minimum of $^{1}/_{4}$ unit vertical in 12 units horizontal (2% slope) for drainage. (Sec. 1402.3)

Flashing

Exterior openings exposed to the weather shall be flashed in such a manner as to make them weatherproof. (Sec. 1402.2)

Exterior Wall Coverings

Except as otherwise noted, the minimum thicknesses of the following exterior wall coverings are based on a maximum stud spacing of 16 inches (406 mm).

Siding. Solid wood siding shall have an average thickness of $^{3}/_{8}$ inch (9.5 mm) unless placed over sheathing.

Siding patterns known as rustic, drop siding, or shiplap shall have an average thickness in place of not less than $^{19}/_{32}$ inch (15 mm) and shall have a minimum thickness of not less than $^{3}/_{8}$ inch (9.5 mm). Bevel siding shall have a minimum thickness measured at the butt section of not less than $^{7}/_{16}$ inch (11 mm) and a tip thickness of not less than $^{3}/_{16}$ inch (4.8 mm). Siding of lesser dimensions may be used, provided such wall covering is placed over approved sheathing.

All weatherboarding or siding shall be securely nailed to each stud with not less than one nail, or to solid 1-inch (25 mm) nominal wood sheathing or $^{15}/_{32}$-inch (12 mm) wood structural panel sheathing or $^{1}/_{2}$-inch (13 mm) particleboard sheathing with not less than one line of nails spaced not more than 24 inches (610 mm) on center in each piece of the weatherboarding or siding. (Sec. 2310.2)

Wood board sidings applied horizontally, diagonally or vertically shall be fastened to studs, nailing strips or blocking set at a maximum 24 inches (610 mm) on center. Fasteners shall be nails or screws with a penetration of not less than $1^1/_2$ inches (38 mm) into studs, studs and wood sheathing combined, or blocking. Distance between such fastenings shall not exceed 24 inches (610 mm) for horizontally or vertically applied sidings, and 32 inches (813 mm) for diagonally applied sidings.

Plywood. Where plywood is used for covering the exterior of outside walls, it shall be of the exterior type not less than $^3/_8$ inch (9.5 mm) thick. Plywood panel siding shall be installed in accordance with Table 23-II-A-1. Unless applied over 1-inch (25 mm) wood sheathing or $^{15}/_{32}$-inch (12 mm) wood structural panel sheathing or $^1/_2$-inch (13 mm) particleboard sheathing, joints shall occur over framing members and shall be protected with a continuous wood batten, approved caulking, flashing, vertical or horizontal shiplaps; or joints shall be lapped horizontally or otherwise made waterproof. (Sec. 2310.3)

Shingles or Shakes. Wood shingles or shakes and asbestos cement shingles may be used for exterior wall covering. All shingles or shakes attached to sheathing other than wood sheathing shall be secured with approved corrosion-resistant fasteners or on furring strips attached to the studs. Wood shingles or shakes may be applied over fiberboard shingle backer and sheathing with annular grooved nails. The thickness of wood shingles or shakes between wood nailing boards shall not be less than $^3/_8$ inch (9.5 mm). Wood shingles or shakes and asbestos shingles or siding may be nailed directly to approved fiberboard nailbase sheathing not less than $^1/_2$-inch (13 mm) nominal thickness with annular grooved nails. The weather exposure of wood shingle or shake siding used on exterior walls shall not exceed maximums set forth in Table 23-II-K. (Sec. 2310.4)

Particleboard. When particleboard is used for covering the exterior of outside walls, it shall be of the M-1, M-S and M-2 Exterior Glue grades. Particleboard panel siding shall be installed in accordance with Tables 23-II-A-2 and 23-II-B-1. Panels shall be gapped $^1/_8$ inch (3.2 mm) and nails shall not be spaced less than $^3/_8$ inch (9.5 mm) from edges and ends of sheathing. Unless applied over $^5/_8$-inch (16 mm) net wood sheathing, $^1/_2$-inch (13 mm) wood structural panel sheathing or $^1/_2$-inch (13 mm) particleboard sheathing, joints shall occur over framing members and shall be covered with a continuous wood batt, or joints shall be lapped horizontally or otherwise made waterproof to the satisfaction of the building official. Particleboard shall be sealed and protected with exterior quality finishes. (Sec. 2310.5)

Hardboard. When hardboard siding is used for covering the outside of exterior walls, it shall be installed in accordance with Table 23-II-C. Lap siding shall be installed horizontally and applied to sheathed or unsheathed walls.

Square-edged nongrooved panels and shiplap grooved or nongrooved siding shall be applied vertically to sheathed or unsheathed walls. Siding that is grooved shall not be less than $^1/_4$ inch (6.4 mm) thick in the groove.

Nail size and spacing shall follow Table 23-II-C and shall penetrate framing $1^1/_2$ inches (38 mm). Lap siding shall overlap 1 inch (25 mm) minimum and be nailed through both courses and into framing members with nails located $^1/_2$ inch (13 mm) from the bottom of the overlapped course. Square-edged nongrooved panels shall be nailed $^3/_8$ inch (9.5 mm) from the perimeter of the panel and intermediately into studs. Shiplap edge panel siding with $^3/_8$-inch (9.5 mm) shiplap shall be nailed $^3/_8$ inch (9.5 mm) from the edges on both sides of the shiplap. The $^3/_4$-inch (19 mm) shiplap shall be nailed $^3/_8$ inch (9.5 mm) from the edge and penetrate through both the overlap and underlap. Top and bottom edges of the panel shall be nailed $^3/_8$ inch (9.5 mm) from the edge.

Shiplap and lap siding shall not be force fit. Square-edged panels shall maintain a $^1/_{16}$-inch (1.6 mm) gap at joints. All joints and edges of siding shall be over framing members and shall be made resistant to weather penetration with battens, horizontal overlaps or shiplaps to the satisfaction of the building official. A $^1/_8$-inch (3.2 mm) gap shall be provided around all openings. (Sec. 2310.6)

Nailing. All fasteners used for the attachment of siding shall be of a corrosion-resistant type. (Sec. 2310.7)

Exterior Plastering

See page 12 for a discussion of exterior plastering.

VENEERED WALLS

(See Figure 10.)

Height

Exterior veneer shall not be attached to wood-frame construction at a point more than 30 feet (9144 mm) in height above the noncombustible foundation, except the 30-foot (9144 mm) limit may be increased when special construction is designed to provide for differential movement and when approved by the building official. (Sec. 1403.1.2)

Vertical Loads

Veneer shall not support any vertical load other than the dead load of the veneer above. Veneer above openings shall be supported upon lintels of noncombustible material. (Secs. 1403.4.1 and 1403.6.2)

Adhered Veneer

One of the following application methods may be used for adhered veneer:

1. A paste of neat portland cement shall be brushed on the backing and the back of the veneer unit. Type S mortar shall then be applied to the backing and the veneer unit. Sufficient mortar shall be used to create a slight excess to be forced out between the edges of the units. The units shall be tapped into place so as to completely fill the space between the units and the backing. The resulting thickness of mortar in back of the units shall not be less than $^1/_2$ inch (12.7 mm) or more than $1^1/_4$ inch (32 mm).

2. Units of tile, masonry, stone or terra cotta, not over 1 inch (25 mm) in thickness, shall be restricted to 81 square inches (52 258 mm^2) in area unless the back side of each unit is ground or box screeded to true up any deviation from plane. These units and glass mosaic units of tile not over 2 inches by 2 inches by $^3/_8$ inch (51 mm by 51 mm by 9.5 mm) in size may be adhered by means of portland cement. Backing may be of masonry, concrete or portland cement plaster on metal lath. Metal lath shall be fastened to the supports in accordance with the requirements for lathing. Type S mortar shall be applied to the backing as a setting bed. The set-

ting bed shall be a minimum of $^3/_8$ inch (9.5 mm) thick and a maximum of $^3/_4$ inch (19 mm) thick. A paste of neat portland cement or half portland cement and half fine-graded sand shall be applied to the back of the exterior veneer units and to the setting bed and the veneer pressed and tapped into place to provide complete coverage between the mortar bed and veneer unit. A cement mortar shall be used to point the veneer. (Sec. 1403.5.4)

Anchored Veneer

Masonry and stone units [5 inches (127 mm) maximum in thickness]: Masonry and stone veneer not exceeding 5 inches (127 mm) in thickness may be anchored directly to structural masonry concrete or studs in one of the following manners:

1. Wall ties shall be corrosion resistant and, if made of sheet metal, shall have a minimum size of 0.030 inch (0.76 mm) (No. 22 galvanized sheet gage) by $^3/_4$ inch (19.1 mm) or, if of wire, shall be a minimum diameter of 0.148 inch (3.76 mm) (No. 9 B.W. gage). Wall ties shall be spaced so as to support not more than 2 square feet (0.19 m^2) of wall area, but not more than 24 inches (610 mm) on center horizontally. In Seismic Zones 3 and 4, wall ties shall have a lip or hook on the extended leg that will engage or enclose a horizontal joint reinforcement wire having a diameter of 0.148 inch (3.76 mm) (No. 9 B.W. gage) or equivalent. The joint reinforcement shall be continuous with butt splices between ties permitted.

When applied over stud construction, the studs shall be spaced a maximum of 16 inches (406 mm) on center, and approved paper shall first be applied over the sheathing or wires between studs, and mortar shall be slushed into the 1-inch (25 mm) space between facing and paper.

As an alternate, an air space of at least 1 inch (25 mm) may be maintained between the backing and the veneer, in which case temporary spot bedding may be used away from the ties to align the veneer. Spot bedding at the ties shall be of cement mortar entirely surrounding the ties.

2. Veneer may be applied with a 1-inch-minimum (25 mm) grouted backing space which is reinforced by not less than 2-inch by 2-inch (51 mm by 51 mm) 0.065 inch (1.65 mm) (No. 16 B.W. gage) galvanized wire mesh placed over waterproof paper backing and anchored directly to stud construction.

The stud spacing shall not exceed 16 inches (406 mm) on center. The galvanized wire mesh shall be anchored to wood studs by galvanized steel wire furring nails at 4 inches (102 mm) on center or by barbed galvanized nails at 6 inches (152 mm) on center with a $1^1/_8$-inch-minimum (29 mm) penetration. The galvanized wire mesh may be attached to steel studs by equivalent wire ties. If this method is applied over solid sheathing, the mesh must be furred for embedment in grout. The wire mesh must be attached at the top and bottom with not less than 8-penny (64 mm) common wire nails. The grout fill shall be placed to fill the space intimately around the mesh and veneer facing. (Sec. 1403.6.4.2)

Support

Anchored veneers shall be supported on footings, foundations or other noncombustible support except as provided under Section 2307, Exception 3.

In Seismic Zones 2, 3 and 4, the weight of all anchored veneers installed on structures more than 30 feet (9144 mm) in height above the noncombustible foundation or support shall be supported by noncombustible, corrosion-resistant structural framing. The structural framing shall have horizontal supports spaced not more than 12 feet (3658 mm) vertically above the initial 30-foot (9144 mm) height. The vertical spacing between horizontal supports may be increased when special design techniques, approved by the building official, are used in the construction.

Noncombustible, noncorrosive lintels and noncombustible supports shall be provided over all openings where the veneer unit is not self-spanning. The deflections of all structural lintels and horizontal supports shall not exceed $^1/_{600}$ of the span under full load of the veneer. (Secs. 1403.6.2 and 2307)

PLASTERING AND INSTALLATION OF WALLBOARD LATHING

Application

The thickness, spacing of supports and method of attachment of lath shall be as set forth in Tables 25-B and 25-C.

Gypsum Lath (See Figure 11.)

Gypsum lath shall be applied with the long dimension perpendicular to supports and with end joints staggered in successive courses. End joints may occur on one support when stripping is applied the full length of the joints.

Where lath edges are not in moderate contact and have joint gaps exceeding $^3/_8$ inch (9.5 mm), the joint gaps shall be covered with stripping or cornerite. Stripping or cornerite may be omitted when the entire surface is reinforced with not less than 1-inch (25 mm) 0.035 inch (0.89 mm) (No. 20 B.W. gage) woven wire. When lath is secured to horizontal or vertical supports not used as structural diaphragms, end joints may occur between supports when lath ends are secured together with approved fasteners. (Sec. 2505.2)

Stripping

Stripping is to be at least 3 inches (76 mm) wide and consists of a flat reinforcing unit of expanded metal or wire fabric. (Sec. 2501.4)

Cornerite

Cornerite is a shaped reinforcing unit of expanded metal or wire fabric with legs at least 2 inches (51 mm) wide. (Sec. 2501.4)

Cornerite shall be installed so as to retain position during plastering at all internal corners. Cornerite may be omitted when plaster is not continuous from one plane to an adjacent plane. (Sec. 2505.2)

Metal Plaster Bases

Metal lath shall be attached to metal supports with not less than 0.049 inch (1.2 mm) (No. 18 B.W. gage) tie wire spaced not more than 6 inches (152 mm) apart or with approved equivalent attachments.

Metal lath or wire fabric lath shall be applied with the long dimension of the sheets perpendicular to supports.

Cornerite shall be installed in all internal corners to retain position during plastering. Cornerite may be omitted when lath is continuous or when plaster is not continuous from one plane to an adjacent plane.

Metal lath shall be lapped not less than $^1/_2$ inch (12.7 mm) at sides and 1 inch (25 mm) at ends. Wire fabric lath shall be lapped not less than one mesh at sides and ends, but not less than 1 inch (25 mm). Rib metal lath with edge ribs greater than $^1/_8$ inch (3 mm) shall be lapped at sides by nesting outside ribs. When edge ribs are $^1/_8$ inch (3 mm) or less, rib metal lath may be lapped $^1/_2$ inch (13 mm) at sides, or outside ribs may be nested. Where end laps of sheets do not occur over supports, they shall be securely tied together with not less than 0.049 inch (1.2 mm) (No. 18 B.W. gage) wire. (Sec. 2505.3)

Exterior Surfaces

All lath and lath attachments used on exterior exposed surfaces shall be corrosion resistant. (Sec. 2506.2)

Gypsum lath or gypsum board shall not be used on weather-exposed surfaces. (Sec. 2511.1)

A minimum 0.019-inch (0.48 mm) (No. 26 galvanized sheet gage) corrosion-resistant weep screed with a minimum vertical attachment flange of $3^1/_2$ inches (89 mm) shall be provided at or below the foundation plate line on all exterior stud walls. The screed shall be placed a minimum of 4 inches (102 mm) above the earth or 2 inches (51 mm) above paved areas and shall be of a type which will allow trapped water to drain to the exterior of the building. The weather-resistive barrier shall lap the attachment flange and exterior lath shall cover and terminate on the attachment flange of the screed. (Sec. 2506.5)

Building Paper

An approved weather-resistive paper shall be applied over studs or sheathing of all exterior walls. Such paper shall be applied weatherboard fashion. See Figure 12. (Sec. 1402.1)

PLASTERING

Interior

General. Plastering with gypsum plaster or cement plaster shall not be less than three coats when applied over metal lath or wire fabric lath and shall not be less than two coats when applied over other bases. (Sec. 2507.1)

Plaster shall not be applied directly to fiber insulation board. Cement plaster shall not be applied directly to gypsum lath, gypsum masonry or gypsum plaster on walls.

When installed, grounds shall assure the minimum thickness of plaster as set forth in Table 25-D. Plaster thickness shall be measured from the face of lath and other bases.

Base coat proportions. Proportions of aggregate to cementitious materials shall not exceed the volume set forth in Table 25-E for gypsum plaster and Table 25-F for cement plaster. (Sec. 2507.2)

Base coat application. Base coats shall be applied with sufficient material and pressure to form a complete key or bond. (Sec. 2507.3.1)

Gypsum plaster. For two-coat work, the first coat shall be brought out to grounds and straightened to a true surface leaving the surface rough to receive the finish coat. For three-coat work, the surface of the first coat shall be scored sufficiently to provide adequate bond for the second coat and shall be permitted to harden and set before the second coat is applied. The second coat shall be brought out to grounds and straightened to a true surface leaving the surface rough to receive the finish coat. (Sec. 2507.3.2)

Cement plaster. The first two coats shall be as required for the first coats of exterior plaster, except that the moist-curing time period between the first and second coats shall not be less than 24 hours and the thickness shall be as set forth in Table 25-D. Moist curing shall not be required where job and weather conditions are favorable to the retention of moisture in the portland cement plaster for the required time period. (Sec. 2507.3.3)

Finish coat application. Finish coats shall be applied with sufficient material and pressure to form a complete bond. Finish coats shall be proportioned and mixed in an approved manner. Gypsum and lime and other interior finish coats shall be applied over gypsum base coats which have hardened and set. Thicknesses shall not be less than $^1/_{16}$ inch (1.6 mm).

Cement plaster finish coats may be applied over interior cement plaster base coats which have been in place not less than 24 hours.

Approved acoustical finish plaster may be applied over any base coat plaster, over clean masonry or concrete, or other approved surfaces. (Sec. 2507.4)

Exterior

General. Plastering with cement plaster shall not be less than three coats when applied over metal lath or wire fabric lath and shall not be less than two coats when applied over masonry or concrete. If plaster surface is completely covered by veneer or other facing material, or is completely concealed by another wall, plaster application need be only two coats, provided the total thickness is as set forth in Table 25-F. (Sec. 2508.1)

Base coat application. The first coat shall be applied with sufficient material and pressure to solidly fill all openings in the lath. The surface shall be scored horizontally sufficiently rough to provide adequate bond to receive the second coat.

The second coat shall be brought out to proper thickness, rodded and floated sufficiently rough to provide adequate bond for the finish coat. The second coat shall have no variation greater than $^1/_4$ inch (6.4 mm) in any direction under a 5-foot (1524 mm) straightedge. (Sec. 2508.3)

Environmental conditions. Portland cement-based plaster shall not be applied to frozen base or those bases containing frost. Plaster mixes shall not contain frozen ingredients. Plaster coats shall be protected from freezing for a period of not less than 24 hours after set has occurred. (Sec. 2508.4)

Curing and interval. First and second coats of plaster shall be applied and moist cured as set forth in Table 25-F. (Sec. 2508.5)

When applied over gypsum backing or directly to unit masonry surfaces, the second coat may be applied as soon as the first coat has attained sufficient hardness.

Finish coats. Finish coats shall be proportioned and mixed in an approved manner and in accordance with Table 25-F.

Cement plaster finish coats shall be applied over base coats which have been in place for the time periods set forth in Table 25-F. (Sec. 2508.7)

WALLBOARD

Gypsum Wallboard

General. Gypsum wallboard shall not be installed on exterior surfaces. Gypsum wallboard shall not be installed until weather protection for the installation is provided. (Sec. 2511.1)

Supports. Supports for wallboard shall be spaced not to exceed the spacing set forth in Table 25-G for single-ply application and Table 25-H for two-ply application. (Sec. 2511.2)

Single-ply application. All edges and ends of gypsum wallboard shall occur on the framing members, except those edges and ends which are perpendicular to the framing members. All edges and ends of gypsum wallboard shall be in moderate contact except in concealed spaces where fire-resistive construction or diaphragm action is not required.

The size and spacing of fasteners shall comply with Table 25-G. Fasteners shall be spaced not less than $^{3}/_{8}$ inch (9.5 mm) from edges and ends of gypsum wallboard. Fasteners at the top and bottom plates of vertical assemblies, or the edges and ends of horizontal assemblies perpendicular to supports, and at the wall line, may be omitted except on shear-resisting elements or fire-resistive assemblies. Fasteners shall be applied in such a manner so as not to fracture the face paper with the fastener head.

Gypsum wallboard may be applied to wood-framing members with an approved adhesive. A continuous bead of the adhesive shall be applied to the face of all framing members, except top and bottom plates, of sufficient size as to spread to an average width of 1 inch (25 mm) and thickness of $^{1}/_{16}$ inch (1.6 mm) when the gypsum wallboard is applied. Where the edges or ends of two pieces of gypsum wallboard occur on the same framing member, two continuous parallel beads of adhesive shall be applied to the framing member. Fasteners shall be used with adhesive application in accordance with Table 25-G. (Sec. 2511.3)

Two-ply application. The base ply of gypsum wallboard shall be applied with fasteners of the type and size as required for the non-adhesive application of single-ply gypsum wallboard. Fastener spacings shall be in accordance with Table 25-H.

The face ply of gypsum wallboard may be applied with gypsum wallboard joint compound or approved adhesive furnishing full coverage between the plies, or with fasteners in accordance with Table 25-H. When the face ply is installed with joint compound or adhesive, the joints of the face ply need not occur on supports. Temporary nails or shoring shall be used to hold face ply in position until the joint compound or adhesive develops adequate bond. (Sec. 2511.4)

Joint treatment. Gypsum wallboard single-layer fire-rated assemblies shall have joints treated.

> **EXCEPTION:** Joint treatment need not be provided when any of the following conditions occur:
>
> 1. Where the wallboard is to receive a decorative finish such as wood paneling, battens, acoustical finishes or any similar application which would be equivalent to joint treatment.
> 2. Joints over wood-framing members.
> 3. Assemblies tested without joint treatment.

(Sec. 2511.5)

INTERIOR PANELING

All softwood wood structural panels shall be installed in accordance with Table 23-II-B-1. (Sec. 2311)

ROOF COVERINGS

General

The roof coverings specified below are permissible for dwellings.

In areas subject to wind-driven snow or roof ice buildup, underlayment consisting of two layers of nonperforated Type 15 felt applied shingle fashion shall be installed and solid mopped together with approved cementing material between the plies extending from the eave up the roof to a point 24 inches (610 mm) inside the exterior wall line of the building.

> **EXCEPTIONS:** 1. For wood shingle or wood shake roofs, the underlayment shall extend 36 inches (914 mm) inside the exterior wall line of the building.
>
> 2. When interlocking tiles are used, the underlayment may consist of one layer of Type 30 or heavier asphalt-coated base sheet except that extending from the eaves up to a point 24 inches (610 mm) inside the exterior wall line of the building, two layers of the underlayment shall be applied shingle fashion and solid cemented together with approved cementing material. When this method is used, all horizontal seams of the base sheet shall be lapped 2 inches (51 mm) and vertical seams of the base sheet shall be lapped 6 inches (152 mm) and be continuously sealed with approved cementing material and shall be applied only over solid sheathing.

Wood Shingles

Each bundle of wood shingles for roofs shall bear the label of an approved inspection bureau or agency. (Sec. 1507.2)

Shingles may be applied to roofs with solid or spaced sheathing. (Table 15-B-2)

All wood shingles shall be laid with a side lap of at least $1^{1}/_{2}$ inches (38 mm) in adjacent courses, and not in direct alignment in alternate courses. (Table 15-B-2)

Every wood shingle shall be laid approximately $^{1}/_{4}$ inch (6.4 mm) from an adjacent shingle and shall be nailed to the sheathing with two corrosion-resistant nails only, positioned approximately $^{3}/_{4}$ inch (19 mm) from each edge and approximately 1 inch (25 mm) above the exposure line. Starter course at the eaves shall be doubled. (Table 15-B-2)

Weather exposures shall not exceed those set forth in Table 15-C. Hip and ridge weather exposures shall not exceed those permitted for the field of the roof. (Table 15-B-2)

Shingles shall not be installed on a roof having a slope less than 3 units vertical in 12 units horizontal (25% slope). (Table 15-B-2)

Wood Shakes

Each bundle of wood shakes shall bear the label of an approved inspection bureau or agency. (Sec. 1507.2)

Shakes may be applied to roofs with solid or spaced sheathing. In wind-driven snow areas, sheathing shall be solid and the shakes shall be applied over an underlayment of not less than nonperforated Type 15 felt applied shingle fashion. (Table 15-B-2)

Shakes shall be laid with a side lap of not less than $1^1/_2$ inches (38 mm) between joints in adjacent courses. Spacing between shakes shall not be less than $^3/_8$ inch (9.5 mm) nor more than $^5/_8$ inch (16 mm), except for preservative-treated wood shakes, which shall have a spacing of not less than $^1/_4$ inch (6.4 mm) nor more than $^3/_8$ inch (9.5 mm).

Shakes shall be fastened to the sheathing with two nails only, positioned approximately 1 inch (25 mm) from each edge and approximately 2 inches (51 mm) above the exposure line. The starter course at the eaves shall be doubled. The bottom or first layer may be either shakes or shingles.

Fifteen-inch or 18-inch (381 mm or 457 mm) shakes may be used for the starter course at the eaves and the final course at the ridge.

Shakes shall be laid with not less than 18-inch-wide (457 mm) interlayment of Type 30 felt shingled between each course in such a manner that no felt is exposed to the weather below the shake butts and in the keyways (between the shakes). (Table 15-B-2)

Weather exposures shall not exceed those set forth in Table 15-C. Hip and ridge weather exposures shall not exceed those permitted for the field of the roof. (Table 15-B-2)

Shakes shall not be installed on a roof having a slope less than 4 units vertical in 12 units horizontal (33.3% slope). (Table 15-B-2)

Asphalt Shingles

Each package of asphalt shingles for roofs shall bear the label of an approved agency having a service for the inspection of material and finished products during manufacture. (Sec. 1507.2)

Asphalt shingles shall be fastened according to manufacturer's instructions to solidly sheathed roofs, but not less than four nails per each 36-inch to 40-inch (914 mm to 1016 mm) strip shingle, and two nails per each individual shingle 9 inches to 18 inches (229 mm to 457 mm) wide shall be used. (Table 15-B-1)

Underlayment of not less than one layer nonperforated Type 15 felt, lapped horizontally and vertically so as to shed water, shall be applied under all asphalt shingles. (Table 15-B-1)

Shingles shall not be installed on a roof having a slope less than 4 units vertical in 12 units horizontal (33.3% slope) except that asphalt shingles may be installed on slopes as low as 2 units vertical in 12 units horizontal (16.7% slope), provided the shingles are approved self-sealing or are hand-sealed and are installed with an underlayment consisting of two layers of nonperforated Type 15 felt applied shingle fashion. (Table 15-B-1)

VALLEY FLASHING

Wood Shingles and Wood Shakes

The roof valley flashing shall be provided of not less than 0.016 inch (0.41 mm) (No. 28 galvanized sheet gage) corrosion-resistant metal applied over an underlayment of not less than Type 15 felt. The metal shall extend at least 8 inches (203 mm) from the center line each way for wood shingles and 11 inches (279 mm) from the center line each way for wood shakes. Sections of flashing shall have an overlap of not less than 4 inches (102 mm). (Sec. 1508.5)

Asphalt Shingles

The roof valley flashing shall be the same as required for wood shingles or shall be of woven asphalt shingles applied in an approved manner with an underlayment of not less than Type 15 felt extending 18 inches (457 mm) from the center line each way. (Sec. 1508.2)

ATTIC ACCESS AND VENTILATION

An access opening shall be provided to attics of buildings with combustible ceiling or roof construction. The opening shall be located in a corridor, hallway or other readily accessible location. Attics with a maximum vertical height of less than 30 inches (762 mm) need not be provided with access openings.

The opening shall not be less than 22 inches by 30 inches (559 mm by 762 mm).

Thirty-inch-minimum (762 mm) clear headroom in the attic space shall be provided at or above the access opening. (Sec. 1505.1)

Where determined necessary by the building official due to atmospheric or climatic conditions, enclosed attics and enclosed rafter spaces formed where ceilings are applied directly to the underside of roof rafters shall have cross ventilation for each separate space by ventilating openings protected against the entrance of rain and snow. Where eave or cornice vents are installed, insulation shall not block the free flow of air. A minimum of 1 inch (25 mm) of air space shall be provided between the insulation and the roof sheathing. The net free ventilating area shall not be less than $^1/_{150}$ of the area of the space ventilated.

EXCEPTIONS: 1. The area may be $^1/_{300}$ of the area of the space ventilated provided 50 percent of the required opening area is provided by ventilators located in the upper portion of the space to be ventilated at least 3 feet (914 mm) above eave or cornice vents with the balance of the required ventilation provided by eave or cornice vents

2. The area may be $^1/_{300}$ of the area of the space ventilated provided a vapor barrier not exceeding 1 perm (5.7×10^{-11} kg/Pa·s·m^2) is installed on the warm side of the attic insulation.

Where eave or cornice vents are installed, insulation shall not block the free flow of air. A minimum of 1 inch (25 mm) of air space shall be provided between the insulation and roof sheathing.

Openings for ventilation shall be covered with corrosion-resistant metal mesh with mesh openings of $^1/_4$ inch (6.4 mm) in dimension.

The openings shall be covered with corrosion-resistant metal mesh with mesh openings of $^1/_4$ inch (6.4 mm) in dimension. (Sec. 1505.3)

GLASS AND GLAZING

Glazing in locations subject to human impact such as glass doors; glazing immediately adjacent to such doors, pool and spa barriers, stairway landings; glazing adjacent to any surface normally used as walking surface; sliding glass door units, including fixed glass panels which are part of such units; shower doors; tub enclosures; and storm doors shall be of safety glazing materials. Safety glazing materials are those so constructed, treated or combined with other materials as to minimize the likelihood of cutting and piercing injuries resulting from human contact with this glazing material and include such materials as laminated glass, tempered glass, wired glass and safety plastic. (Sec. 2406)

TABLE 15-C—MAXIMUM WEATHER EXPOSURE

GRADE LENGTH	3 UNITS VERTICAL TO LESS THAN 4 UNITS VERTICAL IN 12 UNITS HORIZONTAL (25% ≤ 33.3% SLOPE)	4 UNITS VERTICAL IN 12 UNITS HORIZONTAL (33.3% SLOPE)
	× 25.4 for mm	
	Wood Shingles	
1. No. 1 16-inch	3 3/4	5
2. No. 2[1] 16-inch	3 1/2	4
3. No. 3[1] 16-inch	3	3 1/2
4. No. 1 18-inch	4 1/4	5 1/2
5. No. 2[1] 18-inch	4	4 1/2
6. No. 3[1] 18-inch	3 1/2	4
7. No. 1 24-inch	5 3/4	7 1/2
8. No. 2[1] 24-inch	5 1/2	6 1/2
9. No. 3[1] 24-inch	5	5 1/2
	Wood Shakes[2]	
10. No. 1 18-inch	7 1/2	7 1/2
11. No. 1 24-inch	10	10
12. No. 2 18-inch tapersawn shakes	—	5 1/2
13. No. 2 24-inch tapersawn shakes	—	7 1/2

[1]To be used only when specifically permitted by the building official.
[2]Exposure of 24-inch by 3/8-inch (610 mm by 9.5 mm) resawn handsplit shakes shall not exceed 5 inches (127 mm) regardless of the roof slope.

TABLE 23-II-A-1—EXPOSED PLYWOOD PANEL SIDING

MINIMUM THICKNESS[1] (inch)	MINIMUM NUMBER OF PLIES	STUD SPACING (inches) PLYWOOD SIDING APPLIED DIRECTLY TO STUDS OR OVER SHEATHING
× 25.4 for mm		× 25.4 for mm
3/8	3	16[2]
1/2	4	24

[1]Thickness of grooved panels is measured at bottom of grooves.
[2]May be 24 inches (610 mm) if plywood siding applied with face grain perpendicular to studs or over one of the following: (1) 1-inch (25 mm) board sheathing, (2) 7/16-inch (11 mm) wood structural panel sheathing or (3) 3/8-inch (9.5 mm) wood structural panel sheathing with strength axis (which is the long direction of the panel unless otherwise marked) of sheathing perpendicular to studs.

TABLE 23-II-A-2—ALLOWABLE SPANS FOR EXPOSED PARTICLEBOARD PANEL SIDING

GRADE	STUD SPACING (inches)	MINIMUM THICKNESS (inches)		
		× 25.4 for mm		
		Siding		Exterior Ceilings and Soffits
	× 25.4 for mm	Direct to Studs	Continuous Support	Direct to Supports
M-1 M-S M-2 "Exterior Glue"	16 24	5/8 5/8	3/8 3/8	3/8 3/8

TABLE 23-II-B-1—NAILING SCHEDULE

CONNECTION	NAILING[1]
1. Joist to sill or girder, toenail	3-8d
2. Bridging to joist, toenail each end	2-8d
3. 1″ × 6″ (25 mm × 152 mm) subfloor or less to each joist, face nail	2-8d
4. Wider than 1″ × 6″ (25 mm × 152 mm) subfloor to each joist, face nail	3-8d
5. 2″ (51 mm) subfloor to joist or girder, blind and face nail	2-16d
6. Sole plate to joist or blocking, typical face nail Sole plate to joist or blocking, at braced wall panels	16d at 16″ (406 mm) o.c. 3-16d per 16″ (406 mm)
7. Top plate to stud, end nail	2-16d
8. Stud to sole plate	4-8d, toenail or 2-16d, end nail
9. Double studs, face nail	16d at 24″ (610 mm) o.c.
10. Doubled top plates, typical face nail Double top plates, lap splice	16d at 16″ (406 mm) o.c. 8-16d
11. Blocking between joists or rafters to top plate, toenail	3-8d
12. Rim joist to top plate, toenail	8d at 6″ (152 mm) o.c.
13. Top plates, laps and intersections, face nail	2-16d
14. Continuous header, two pieces	16d at 16″ (406 mm) o.c. along each edge
15. Ceiling joists to plate, toenail	3-8d
16. Continuous header to stud, toenail	4-8d
17. Ceiling joists, laps over partitions, face nail	3-16d
18. Ceiling joists to parallel rafters, face nail	3-16d
19. Rafter to plate, toenail	3-8d
20. 1″ (25 mm) brace to each stud and plate, face nail	2-8d
21. 1″ × 8″ (25 mm × 203 mm) sheathing or less to each bearing, face nail	2-8d
22. Wider than 1″ × 8″ (25 mm × 203 mm) sheathing to each bearing, face nail	3-8d
23. Built-up corner studs	16d at 24″ (610 mm) o.c.
24. Built-up girder and beams	20d at 32″ (813 mm) o.c. at top and bottom and staggered 2-20d at ends and at each splice
25. 2″ (51 mm) planks	2-16d at each bearing
26. Wood structural panels and particleboard[2]: Subfloor and wall sheathing (to framing): 1/2″ (12.7 mm) and less 19/32″-3/4″ (15 mm-19 mm) 7/8″-1″ (22 mm-25 mm) 1 1/8″-1 1/4″ (29 mm-32 mm) Combination subfloor-underlayment (to framing): 3/4″ (19 mm) and less 7/8″-1″ (22 mm-25 mm) 1 1/8″-1 1/4″ (29 mm-32 mm)	 6d[3] 8d[4] or 6d[5] 8d[3] 10d[4] or 8d[5] 6d[5] 8d[5] 10d[4] or 8d[5]
27. Panel siding (to framing):[2] 1/2″ (12.7 mm) or less 5/8″ (16 mm)	 6d[6] 8d[6]
28. Fiberboard sheathing:[7] 1/2″ (12.7 mm) 25/32″ (20 mm)	 No. 11 ga.[8] 6d[4] No. 16 ga.[9] No. 11 ga.[8] 8d[4] No. 16 ga.[9]
29. Interior paneling 1/4″ (6.4 mm) 3/8″ (9.5 mm)	 4d[10] 6d[11]

[1]Common or box nails may be used except where otherwise stated.

[2]Nails spaced at 6 inches (152 mm) on center at edges, 12 inches (305 mm) at intermediate supports except 6 inches (152 mm) at all supports where spans are 48 inches (1219 mm) or more. For nailing of wood structural panel and particleboard diaphragms and shear walls, refer to Sections 2315.3.3 and 2315.4. Nails for wall sheathing may be common, box or casing.

[3]Common or deformed shank.

[4]Common.

[5]Deformed shank.

[6]Corrosion-resistant siding or casing nails conforming to the requirements of Section 2304.3.

[7]Fasteners spaced 3 inches (76 mm) on center at exterior edges and 6 inches (152 mm) on center at intermediate supports.

[8]Corrosion-resistant roofing nails with 7/16-inch-diameter (11 mm) head and 1 1/2-inch (38 mm) length for 1/2-inch (12.7 mm) sheathing and 1 3/4-inch (44 mm) length for 25/32-inch (20 mm) sheathing conforming to the requirements of Section 2304.3.

[9]Corrosion-resistant staples with nominal 7/16-inch (11 mm) crown and 1 1/8-inch (29 mm) length for 1/2-inch (12.7 mm) sheathing and 1 1/2-inch (38 mm) length for 25/32-inch (20 mm) sheathing conforming to the requirements of Section 2304.3.

[10]Panel supports at 16 inches (406 mm) [20 inches (508 mm) if strength axis in the long direction of the panel, unless otherwise marked]. Casing or finish nails spaced 6 inches (152 mm) on panel edges, 12 inches (305 mm) at intermediate supports.

[11]Panel supports at 24 inches (610 mm). Casing or finish nails spaced 6 inches (152 mm) on panel edges, 12 inches (305 mm) at intermediate supports.

TABLE 23-II-B-2—WOOD STRUCTURAL PANEL ROOF SHEATHING NAILING SCHEDULE[1]

WIND REGION	NAILS	PANEL LOCATION	ROOF FASTENING ZONE[2] 1	2	3
			Fastening Schedule (inches on center) × 25.4 for mm		
Greater than 90 mph (145 km/h)	8d common	Panel edges[3]	6	6	4[4]
		Panel field	6	6	6[4]
Greater than 80 mph (129 km/h) to 90 mph (145 km/h)	8d common	Panel edges[3]	6	6	4
		Panel field	12	6	6
80 mph (129 km/h) or less	8d common	Panel edges[3]	6	6	6
		Panel field	12	12	12

[1]Applies only to mean roof heights up to 35 feet (10 700 mm). For mean roof heights over 35 feet (10 700 mm), the nailing shall be designed.

[2]The roof fastening zones are shown below:

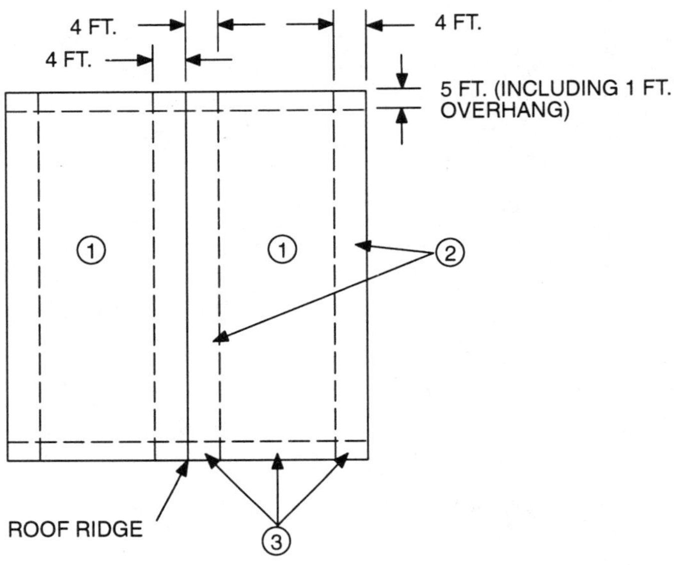

ROOF FASTENING ZONES

For **SI:** 1 foot = 304.8 mm.

[3]Edge spacing also applies over roof framing at gable-end walls.

[4]Use 8d ring-shank nails in this zone if mean roof height is greater than 25 feet (7600 mm).

TABLE 23-II-C—HARDBOARD SIDING

SIDING	MINIMAL NOMINAL THICKNESS (inch)	FRAMING (2″ x 4″) MAXIMUM SPACING	NAIL SIZE[1, 2]	NAIL SPACING General	NAIL SPACING Bracing Panels[3]
	× 25.4 for mm				
1. LAP SIDING					
Direct to studs	3/8	16″ o.c.	8d	16″ o.c.	Not applicable
Over sheathing	3/8	16″ o.c.	10d	16″ o.c.	Not applicable
2. SQUARE EDGE PANEL SIDING					
Direct to studs	3/8	24″ o.c.	6d	6″ o.c. edges; 12″ o.c. at intermed. supports	4″ o.c. edges; 8″ o.c. intermed. supports
Over sheathing	3/8	24″ o.c.	8d	6″ o.c. edges; 12″ o.c. at intermed. supports	4″ o.c. edges; 8″ o.c. intermed. supports
3. SHIPLAP EDGE PANEL SIDING					
Direct to studs	3/8	16″ o.c.	6d	6″ o.c. edges; 12″ o.c. at intermed. supports	4″ o.c. edges; 8″ o.c. intermed. supports
Over sheathing	3/8	16″ o.c.	8d	6″ o.c. edges; 12″ o.c. at intermed. supports	4″ o.c. edges; 8″ o.c. intermed. supports

[1]Nails shall be corrosion resistant in accordance with Division III, Part III.
[2]Minimum acceptable nail dimensions (inches).

	Panel Siding (inch)	Lap Siding (inch)
	× 25.4 for mm	
Shank diameter	0.092	0.099
Head diameter	0.225	0.240

[3]When used to comply with Division IV, Section 2320.11.3.

TABLE 23-II-D-1—ALLOWABLE SPANS FOR LUMBER FLOOR AND ROOF SHEATHING[1, 2]

SPAN (inches)	MINIMUM NET THICKNESS (inches) OF LUMBER PLACED			
	Perpendicular to Supports		Diagonally to Supports	
	× 25.4 for mm			
× 25.4 for mm	Surfaced Dry[3]	Surfaced Unseasoned	Surfaced Dry[3]	Surfaced Unseasoned
Floors				
1. 24	3/4	25/32	3/4	25/32
2. 16	5/8	11/16	5/8	11/16
Roofs				
3. 24	5/8	11/16	3/4	25/32

[1]Installation details shall conform to Sections 2320.9.1 and 2320.12.8 for floor and roof sheathing, respectively.
[2]Floor or roof sheathing conforming with this table shall be deemed to meet the design criteria of Section 2312.
[3]Maximum 19 percent moisture content.

TABLE 23-II-D-2—SHEATHING LUMBER SHALL MEET THE FOLLOWING MINIMUM GRADE REQUIREMENTS: BOARD GRADE

SOLID FLOOR OR ROOF SHEATHING	SPACED ROOF SHEATHING	GRADING RULES
1. Utility	Standard	NLGA, WCLIB, WWPA
2. 4 common or utility	3 common or standard	NLGA, WCLIB, WWPA, NHPMA or NELMA
3. No. 3	No. 2	SPIB
4. Merchantable	Construction common	RIS

TABLE 23-II-E-1—ALLOWABLE SPANS AND LOADS FOR WOOD STRUCTURAL PANEL SHEATHING AND SINGLE-FLOOR GRADES CONTINUOUS OVER TWO OR MORE SPANS WITH STRENGTH AXIS PERPENDICULAR TO SUPPORTS[1,2]

SHEATHING GRADES		ROOF[3]				FLOOR[4]
Panel Span Rating	Panel Thickness (inches)	Maximum Span (inches) × 25.4 for mm		Load[5] (pounds per square foot) × 0.0479 for kN/m²		Maximum Span (inches)
Roof/Floor Span	× 25.4 for mm	With Edge Support[6]	Without Edge Support	Total Load	Live Load	× 25.4 for mm
12/0	5/16	12	12	40	30	0
16/0	5/16, 3/8	16	16	40	30	0
20/0	5/16, 3/8	20	20	40	30	0
24/0	3/8, 7/16, 1/2	24	20[7]	40	30	0
24/16	7/16, 1/2	24	24	50	40	16
32/16	15/32, 1/2, 5/8	32	28	40	30	16[8]
40/20	19/32, 5/8, 3/4, 7/8	40	32	40	30	20[8,9]
48/24	23/32, 3/4, 7/8	48	36	45	35	24
54/32	7/8, 1	54	40	45	35	32
60/48	7/8, 1, 1 1/8	60	48	45	35	48
SINGLE-FLOOR GRADES		**ROOF[3]**				**FLOOR[4]**
Panel Span Rating (inches)	Panel Thickness (inches)	Maximum Span (inches) × 25.4 for mm		Load[5] (pounds per square foot) × 0.0479 for kN/m²		Maximum Span (inches)
× 25.4 for mm		With Edge Support[6]	Without Edge Support	Total Load	Live Load	× 25.4 for mm
16 oc	1/2, 19/32, 5/8	24	24	50	40	16[8]
20 oc	19/32, 5/8, 3/4	32	32	40	30	20[8,9]
24 oc	23/32, 3/4	48	36	35	25	24
32 oc	7/8, 1	48	40	50	40	32
48 oc	1 3/32, 1 1/8	60	48	50	50	48

[1]Applies to panels 24 inches (610 mm) or wider.

[2]Floor and roof sheathing conforming with this table shall be deemed to meet the design criteria of Section 2312.

[3]Uniform load deflection limitations 1/180 of span under live load plus dead load, 1/240 under live load only.

[4]Panel edges shall have approved tongue-and-groove joints or shall be supported with blocking unless 1/4-inch (6.4 mm) minimum thickness underlayment or 1 1/2 inches (38 mm) of approved cellular or lightweight concrete is placed over the subfloor, or finish floor is 3/4-inch (19 mm) wood strip. Allowable uniform load based on deflection of 1/360 of span is 100 pounds per square foot (psf) (4.79 kN/m²) except the span rating of 48 inches on center is based on a total load of 65 psf (3.11 kN/m).

[5]Allowable load at maximum span.

[6]Tongue-and-groove edges, panel edge clips [one midway between each support, except two equally spaced between supports 48 inches (1219 mm) on center], lumber blocking, or other. Only lumber blocking shall satisfy blocked diaphragms requirements.

[7]For 1/2-inch (12.7 mm) panel, maximum span shall be 24 inches (610 mm).

[8]May be 24 inches (610 mm) on center where 3/4-inch (19 mm) wood strip flooring is installed at right angles to joist.

[9]May be 24 inches (610 mm) on center for floors where 1 1/2 inches (38 mm) of cellular or lightweight concrete is applied over the panels.

TABLE 23-II-E-2—ALLOWABLE LOAD (PSF) FOR WOOD STRUCTURAL PANEL ROOF SHEATHING CONTINUOUS OVER TWO OR MORE SPANS AND STRENGTH AXIS PARALLEL TO SUPPORTS (Plywood structural panels are five-ply, five-layer unless otherwise noted.)[1,2]

PANEL GRADE	THICKNESS (inch)	MAXIMUM SPAN (inches)	LOAD AT MAXIMUM SPAN (psf) × 0.0479 for kN/m²	
	× 25.4 for mm		Live	Total
Structural I	7/16	24	20	30
	15/32	24	35[3]	45[3]
	1/2	24	40[3]	50[3]
	19/32, 5/8	24	70	80
	23/32, 3/4	24	90	100
Other grades covered in UBC Standard 23-2 or 23-3	7/16	16	40	50
	15/32	24	20	25
	1/2	24	25	30
	19/32	24	40[3]	50[3]
	5/8	24	45[3]	55[3]
	23/32, 3/4	24	60[3]	65[3]

[1]Roof sheathing conforming with this table shall be deemed to meet the design criteria of Section 2312.

[2]Uniform load deflection limitations: 1/180 of span under live load plus dead load, 1/240 under live load only. Edges shall be blocked with lumber or other approved type of edge supports.

[3]For composite and four-ply plywood structural panel, load shall be reduced by 15 pounds per square foot (0.72 kN/m²).

TABLE 23-II-K—WOOD SHINGLE AND SHAKE SIDE WALL EXPOSURES

SHINGLE OR SHAKE	MAXIMUM WEATHER EXPOSURES (inches) × 25.4 for mm			
	Single-Coursing		Double-Coursing	
Length and Type	No. 1	No. 2	No. 1	No. 2
16-inch (405 mm) shingles	$7\frac{1}{2}$	$7\frac{1}{2}$	12	10
18-inch (455 mm) shingles	$8\frac{1}{2}$	$8\frac{1}{2}$	14	11
24-inch (610 mm) shingles	$11\frac{1}{2}$	$11\frac{1}{2}$	16	14
18-inch (455 mm) resawn shakes	$8\frac{1}{2}$	—	14	—
18-inch (455 mm) straight-split shakes	$8\frac{1}{2}$	—	16	—
24-inch (610 mm) resawn shakes	$11\frac{1}{2}$	—	20	—

TABLE 23-IV-B—SIZE, HEIGHT AND SPACING OF WOOD STUDS

STUD SIZE (inches)	BEARING WALLS				NONBEARING WALLS	
	Laterally Unsupported Stud Height[1] (feet)	Supporting Roof and Ceiling Only	Supporting One Floor, Roof and Ceiling	Supporting Two Floors, Roof and Ceiling	Laterally Unsupported Stud Height[1] (feet)	Spacing (inches)
		Spacing (inches)				
× 25.4 for mm	× 304.8 for mm	× 25.4 for mm			× 304.8 for mm	× 25.4 for mm
1. 2 × 3[2]	—	—	—	—	10	16
2. 2 × 4	10	24	16	—	14	24
3. 3 × 4	10	24	24	16	14	24
4. 2 × 5	10	24	24	—	16	24
5. 2 × 6	10	24	24	16	20	24

[1]Listed heights are distances between points of lateral support placed perpendicular to the plane of the wall. Increases in unsupported height are permitted where justified by an analysis.
[2]Shall not be used in exterior walls.

TABLE 23-IV-C-1—BRACED WALL PANELS[1]

SEISMIC ZONE	CONDITION	CONSTRUCTION METHOD[2,3]								BRACED PANEL LOCATION AND LENGTH[4]
		1	2	3	4	5	6	7	8	
0, 1 and 2A	One story, top of two or three story	X	X	X	X	X	X	X	X	Each end and not more than 25 feet (7620 mm) on center
	First story of two story or second story of three story	X	X	X	X	X	X	X	X	
	First story of three story		X	X	X	X[5]	X	X	X	
2B, 3 and 4	One story, top of two story or three story		X	X	X	X	X	X[6]	X	Each end and not more than 25 feet (7620 mm) on center
	First story of two story or second of three story		X	X	X	X[5]	X	X[6]	X	Each end and not more than 25 feet (7620 mm) on center but not less than 25% of building length[7]
	First story of three story		X	X	X	X[5]	X	X[6]	X	Each end and not more than 25 feet (7620 mm) on center but not less than 40% of building length[7]

[1]This table specifies minimum requirements for braced panels which form interior or exterior braced wall lines.
[2]See Section 2320.11.3 for full description.
[3]See Section 2320.11.4 for alternate braced panel requirement.
[4]Building length is the dimension parallel to the braced wall length.
[5]Gypsum wallboard applied to supports at 16 inches (406 mm) on center.
[6]Not permitted for bracing cripple walls in Seismic Zone 4. See Section 2320.11.5.
[7]The required lengths shall be doubled for gypsum board applied to only one face of a braced wall panel.

TABLE 23-IV-C-2—CRIPPLE WALL BRACING

SEISMIC ZONE	CONDITION	AMOUNT OF CRIPPLE WALL BRACING[1,2] × 25.4 for mm
4	One story above cripple wall	3/8″ wood structural panel with 8d at 6″/12″ nailing on 60 percent of wall length minimum
	Two story above cripple wall	3/8″ wood structural panel with 8d at 4″/12″ nailing on 50 percent of wall length minimum or 3/8″ wood structural panel with 8d at 6″/12″ nailing on 75 percent of wall length minimum
3	One story above cripple wall	3/8″ wood structural panel with 8d at 6″/12″ nailing on 40 percent of wall length minimum
0, 1 and 2	One story above cripple wall	3/8″ wood structural panel with 8d at 6″/12″ nailing on 30 percent of wall length minimum
0, 1, 2 and 3	Two story above cripple wall	3/8″ wood structural panel with 8d at 4″/12″ nailing on 40 percent of wall length minimum or 3/8″ wood structural panel with 8d at 6″/12″ nailing on 60 percent of wall length minimum

[1]Braced panel length shall be at least two times the height of the cripple wall, but not less than 48 inches (1219 mm).

[2]All panels along a wall shall be nearly equal in length and shall be nearly equally spaced along the length of the wall.

TABLE 23-IV-D-2—ALLOWABLE SPANS FOR PARTICLEBOARD WALL SHEATHING[1]
(Not exposed to the weather, long dimension of the panel parallel or perpendicular to studs)

GRADE	THICKNESS (Inch)	STUD SPACING (inches) × 25.4 for mm: Siding Nailed to Studs	Sheathing under Coverings Specified in Section 2326.11.3 Parallel or Perpendicular to Studs
	× 25.4 for mm		
M-1 M-S M-2 "Exterior Glue"	3/8	16	16
	1/2	16	16

[1]In reference to Section 2326.11.3, blocking of horizontal joints is not required.

TABLE 23-IV-J-1—FLOOR JOISTS WITH L/360 DEFLECTION LIMITS
The allowable bending stress (F_b) and modulus of elasticity (E) used in this table shall be from Tables 23-IV-V-1 and 23-IV-V-2 only.

DESIGN CRITERIA:
Deflection — For 40 psf (1.92 kN/m²) live load.
Limited to span in inches (mm) divided by 360.
Strength — Live load of 40 psf (1.92 kN/m²) plus dead load of 10 psf (0.48 kN/m²) determines the required bending design value.

Joist Size (in)	Spacing (in)	Modulus of Elasticity, E, in 1,000,000 psi × 0.00689 for N/mm²																
× 25.4 for mm		0.8	0.9	1.0	1.1	1.2	1.3	1.4	1.5	1.6	1.7	1.8	1.9	2.0	2.1	2.2	2.3	2.4
2 × 6	12.0	8-6	8-10	9-2	9-6	9-9	10-0	10-3	10-6	10-9	10-11	11-2	11-4	11-7	11-9	11-11	12-1	12-3
	16.0	7-9	8-0	8-4	8-7	8-10	9-1	9-4	9-6	9-9	9-11	10-2	10-4	10-6	10-8	10-10	11-0	11-2
	19.2	7-3	7-7	7-10	8-1	8-4	8-7	8-9	9-0	9-2	9-4	9-6	9-8	9-10	10-0	10-2	10-4	10-6
	24.0	6-9	7-0	7-3	7-6	7-9	7-11	8-2	8-4	8-6	8-8	8-10	9-0	9-2	9-4	9-6	9-7	9-9
2 × 8	12.0	11-3	11-8	12-1	12-6	12-10	13-2	13-6	13-10	14-2	14-5	14-8	15-0	15-3	15-6	15-9	15-11	16-2
	16.0	10-2	10-7	11-0	11-4	11-8	12-0	12-3	12-7	12-10	13-1	13-4	13-7	13-10	14-1	14-3	14-6	14-8
	19.2	9-7	10-0	10-4	10-8	11-0	11-3	11-7	11-10	12-1	12-4	12-7	12-10	13-0	13-3	13-5	13-8	13-10
	24.0	8-11	9-3	9-7	9-11	10-2	10-6	10-9	11-0	11-3	11-5	11-8	11-11	12-1	12-3	12-6	12-8	12-10
2 × 10	12.0	14-4	14-11	15-5	15-11	16-5	16-10	17-3	17-8	18-0	18-5	18-9	19-1	19-5	19-9	20-1	20-4	20-8
	16.0	13-0	13-6	14-0	14-6	14-11	15-3	15-8	16-0	16-5	16-9	17-0	17-4	17-8	17-11	18-3	18-6	18-9
	19.2	12-3	12-9	13-2	13-7	14-0	14-5	14-9	15-1	15-5	15-9	16-0	16-4	16-7	16-11	17-2	17-5	17-8
	24.0	11-4	11-10	12-3	12-8	13-0	13-4	13-8	14-0	14-4	14-7	14-11	15-2	15-5	15-8	15-11	16-2	16-5
2 × 12	12.0	17-5	18-1	18-9	19-4	19-11	20-6	21-0	21-6	21-11	22-5	22-10	23-3	23-7	24-0	24-5	24-9	25-1
	16.0	15-10	16-5	17-0	17-7	18-1	18-7	19-1	19-6	19-11	20-4	20-9	21-1	21-6	21-10	22-2	22-6	22-10
	19.2	14-11	15-6	16-0	16-7	17-0	17-6	17-11	18-4	18-9	19-2	19-6	19-10	20-2	20-6	20-10	21-2	21-6
	24.0	13-10	14-4	14-11	15-4	15-10	16-3	16-8	17-0	17-5	17-9	18-1	18-5	18-9	19-1	19-4	19-8	19-11
F_b	12.0	718	777	833	888	941	993	1,043	1,092	1,140	1,187	1,233	1,278	1,323	1,367	1,410	1,452	1,494
	16.0	790	855	917	977	1,036	1,093	1,148	1,202	1,255	1,306	1,357	1,407	1,456	1,504	1,551	1,598	1,644
	19.2	840	909	975	1,039	1,101	1,161	1,220	1,277	1,333	1,388	1,442	1,495	1,547	1,598	1,649	1,698	1,747
	24.0	905	979	1,050	1,119	1,186	1,251	1,314	1,376	1,436	1,496	1,554	1,611	1,667	1,722	1,776	1,829	1,882

NOTE: The required bending design value, F_b, in pounds per square inch (× 0.00689 for N/mm²) is shown at the bottom of this table and is applicable to all lumber sizes shown. Spans are shown in feet-inches (1 foot = 304.8 mm, 1 inch = 25.4 mm) and are limited to 26 feet (7925 mm) and less.

TABLE 23-IV-J-2—FLOOR JOISTS WITH L/360 DEFLECTION LIMITS

The allowable bending stress (F_b) and modulus of elasticity (*E*) used in this table shall be from Tables 23-IV-V-1 and 23-IV-V-2 only.

DESIGN CRITERIA:
Deflection — For 40 psf (1.92 kN/m^2) live load.
Limited to span in inches (mm) divided by 360.
Strength — Live load of 40 psf (1.92 kN/m^2) plus dead load of 20 psf (0.96 kN/m^2) determines the required bending design value.

Joist Size (in)	Spacing (in)	Modulus of Elasticity, *E*, in 1,000,000 psi × 0.00689 for N/mm^2																
× 25.4 for mm		0.8	0.9	1.0	1.1	1.2	1.3	1.4	1.5	1.6	1.7	1.8	1.9	2.0	2.1	2.2	2.3	2.4
2 × 6	12.0	8-6	8-10	9-2	9-6	9-9	10-0	10-3	10-6	10-9	10-11	11-2	11-4	11-7	11-9	11-11	12-1	12-3
	16.0	7-9	8-0	8-4	8-7	8-10	9-1	9-4	9-6	9-9	9-11	10-2	10-4	10-6	10-8	10-10	11-0	11-2
	19.2	7-3	7-7	7-10	8-1	8-4	8-7	8-9	9-0	9-2	9-4	9-6	9-8	9-10	10-0	10-2	10-4	10-6
	24.0	6-9	7-0	7-3	7-6	7-9	7-11	8-2	8-4	8-6	8-8	8-10	9-0	9-2	9-4	9-6	9-7	9-9
2 × 8	12.0	11-3	11-8	12-1	12-6	12-10	13-2	13-6	13-10	14-2	14-5	14-8	15-0	15-3	15-6	15-9	15-11	16-2
	16.0	10-2	10-7	11-0	11-4	11-8	12-0	12-3	12-7	12-10	13-1	13-4	13-7	13-10	14-1	14-3	14-6	14-8
	19.2	9-7	10-0	10-4	10-8	11-0	11-3	11-7	11-10	12-1	12-4	12-7	12-10	13-0	13-3	13-5	13-8	13-10
	24.0	8-11	9-3	9-7	9-11	10-2	10-6	10-9	11-0	11-3	11-5	11-8	11-11	12-1	12-3	12-6	12-8	12-10
2 × 10	12.0	14-4	14-11	15-5	15-11	16-5	16-10	17-3	17-8	18-0	18-5	18-9	19-1	19-5	19-9	20-1	20-4	20-8
	16.0	13-0	13-6	14-0	14-6	14-11	15-3	15-8	16-0	16-5	16-9	17-0	17-4	17-8	17-11	18-3	18-6	18-9
	19.2	12-3	12-9	13-2	13-7	14-0	14-5	14-9	15-1	15-5	15-9	16-0	16-4	16-7	16-11	17-2	17-5	17-8
	24.0	11-4	11-10	12-3	12-8	13-0	13-4	13-8	14-0	14-4	14-7	14-11	15-2	15-5	15-8	15-11	16-2	16-5
2 × 12	12.0	17-5	18-1	18-9	19-4	19-11	20-6	21-0	21-6	21-11	22-5	22-10	23-3	23-7	24-0	24-5	24-9	25-1
	16.0	15-10	16-5	17-0	17-7	18-1	18-7	19-1	19-6	19-11	20-4	20-9	21-1	21-6	21-10	22-2	22-6	22-10
	19.2	14-11	15-6	16-0	16-7	17-0	17-6	17-11	18-4	18-9	19-2	19-6	19-10	20-2	20-6	20-10	21-2	21-6
	24.0	13-10	14-4	14-11	15-4	15-10	16-3	16-8	17-0	17-5	17-9	18-1	18-5	18-9	19-1	19-4	19-8	19-11
F_b	12.0	862	932	1,000	1,066	1,129	1,191	1,251	1,310	1,368	1,424	1,480	1,534	1,587	1,640	1,692	1,742	1,793
	16.0	949	1,026	1,101	1,173	1,243	1,311	1,377	1,442	1,506	1,568	1,629	1,688	1,747	1,805	1,862	1,918	1,973
	19.2	1,008	1,090	1,170	1,246	1,321	1,393	1,464	1,533	1,600	1,666	1,731	1,794	1,857	1,918	1,978	2,038	2,097
	24.0	1,086	1,174	1,260	1,343	1,423	1,501	1,577	1,651	1,724	1,795	1,864	1,933	2,000	2,066	2,131	2,195	2,258

NOTE: The required bending design value, F_b, in pounds per square inch (× 0.00689 for N/mm^2) is shown at the bottom of this table and is applicable to all lumber sizes shown. Spans are shown in feet-inches (1 foot = 304.8 mm, 1 inch = 25.4 mm) and are limited to 26 feet (7925 mm) and less.

TABLE 23-IV-J-3—CEILING JOISTS WITH *L*/240 DEFLECTION LIMITS

The allowable bending stress (F_b) and modulus of elasticity *(E)* used in this table shall be from Tables 23-IV-V-1 and 23-IV-V-2 only.

DESIGN CRITERIA:
Deflection — For 10 psf (0.48 kN/m²) live load.
Limited to span in inches (mm) divided by 240.
Strength — Live load of 10 psf (0.48 kN/mm²) plus dead load of 5 psf (0.24 kN/m²) determines the required fiber stress value.

Joist Size (in)	Spacing (in)	Modulus of Elasticity, *E*, in 1,000,000 psi																
		× 0.00689 for N/mm²																
× 25.4 for mm		0.8	0.9	1.0	1.1	1.2	1.3	1.4	1.5	1.6	1.7	1.8	1.9	2.0	2.1	2.2	2.3	2.4
2 × 4	12.0	9-10	10-3	10-7	10-11	11-3	11-7	11-10	12-2	12-5	12-8	12-11	13-2	13-4	13-7	13-9	14-0	14-2
	16.0	8-11	9-4	9-8	9-11	10-3	10-6	10-9	11-0	11-3	11-6	11-9	11-11	12-2	12-4	12-6	12-9	12-11
	19.2	8-5	8-9	9-1	9-4	9-8	9-11	10-2	10-4	10-7	10-10	11-0	11-3	11-5	11-7	11-9	12-0	12-2
	24.0	7-10	8-1	8-5	8-8	8-11	9-2	9-5	9-8	9-10	10-0	10-3	10-5	10-7	10-9	10-11	11-1	11-3
2 × 6	12.0	15-6	16-1	16-8	17-2	17-8	18-2	18-8	19-1	19-6	19-11	20-3	20-8	21-0	21-4	21-8	22-0	22-4
	16.0	14-1	14-7	15-2	15-7	16-1	16-6	16-11	17-4	17-8	18-1	18-5	18-9	19-1	19-5	19-8	20-0	20-3
	19.2	13-3	13-9	14-3	14-8	15-2	15-7	15-11	16-4	16-8	17-0	17-4	17-8	17-11	18-3	18-6	18-10	19-1
	24.0	12-3	12-9	13-3	13-8	14-1	14-5	14-9	15-2	15-6	15-9	16-1	16-4	16-8	16-11	17-2	17-5	17-8
2 × 8	12.0	20-5	21-2	21-11	22-8	23-4	24-0	24-7	25-2	25-8								
	16.0	18-6	19-3	19-11	20-7	21-2	21-9	22-4	22-10	23-4	23-10	24-3	24-8	25-2	25-7	25-11		
	19.2	17-5	18-1	18-9	19-5	19-11	20-6	21-0	21-6	21-11	22-5	22-10	23-3	23-8	24-0	24-5	24-9	25-2
	24.0	16-2	16-10	17-5	18-0	18-6	19-0	19-6	19-11	20-5	20-10	21-2	21-7	21-11	22-4	22-8	23-0	23-4
2 × 10	12.0	26-0																
	16.0	23-8	24-7	25-5														
	19.2	22-3	23-1	23-11	24-9	25-5												
	24.0	20-8	21-6	22-3	22-11	23-8	24-3	24-10	25-5	26-0								
F_b	12.0	711	769	825	880	932	983	1,033	1,082	1,129	1,176	1,221	1,266	1,310	1,354	1,396	1,438	1,480
	16.0	783	847	909	968	1,026	1,082	1,137	1,191	1,243	1,294	1,344	1,394	1,442	1,490	1,537	1,583	1,629
	19.2	832	900	965	1,029	1,090	1,150	1,208	1,265	1,321	1,375	1,429	1,481	1,533	1,583	1,633	1,682	1,731
	24.0	896	969	1,040	1,108	1,174	1,239	1,302	1,363	1,423	1,481	1,539	1,595	1,651	1,706	1,759	1,812	1,864

NOTE: The required bending design value, F_b, in pounds per square inch (× 0.00689 for N/mm²) is shown at the bottom of this table and is applicable to all lumber sizes shown. Spans are shown in feet-inches (1 foot = 304.8 mm, 1 inch = 25.4 mm) and are limited to 26 feet (7925 mm) and less.

TABLE 23-IV-J-4—CEILING JOISTS WITH *L*/240 DEFLECTION LIMITS

The allowable bending stress (F_b) and modulus of elasticity (*E*) used in this table shall be from Tables 23-IV-V-1 and 23-IV-V-2 only.

DESIGN CRITERIA:
Deflection — For 20 psf (0.96 kN/m^2) live load.
Limited to span in inches (mm) divided by 240.
Strength — Live load of 20 psf (0.96 kN/m^2) plus dead load of 10 psf (0.48 kN/m^2) determines the required bending design value.

Joist Size (in)	Spacing (in)	Modulus of Elasticity, *E*, in 1,000,000 psi × 0.00689 for N/mm^2																
× 25.4 for mm		0.8	0.9	1.0	1.1	1.2	1.3	1.4	1.5	1.6	1.7	1.8	1.9	2.0	2.1	2.2	2.3	2.4
2 × 4	12.0	7-10	8-1	8-5	8-8	8-11	9-2	9-5	9-8	9-10	10-0	10-3	10-5	10-7	10-9	10-11	11-1	11-3
	16.0	7-1	7-5	7-8	7-11	8-1	8-4	8-7	8-9	8-11	9-1	9-4	9-6	9-8	9-9	9-11	10-1	10-3
	19.2	6-8	6-11	7-2	7-5	7-8	7-10	8-1	8-3	8-5	8-7	8-9	8-11	9-1	9-3	9-4	9-6	9-8
	24.0	6-2	6-5	6-8	6-11	7-1	7-3	7-6	7-8	7-10	8-0	8-1	8-3	8-5	8-7	8-8	8-10	8-11
2 × 6	12.0	12-3	12-9	13-3	13-8	14-1	14-5	14-9	15-2	15-6	15-9	16-1	16-4	16-8	16-11	17-2	17-5	17-8
	16.0	11-2	11-7	12-0	12-5	12-9	13-1	13-5	13-9	14-1	14-4	14-7	14-11	15-2	15-5	15-7	15-10	16-1
	19.2	10-6	10-11	11-4	11-8	12-0	12-4	12-8	12-11	13-3	13-6	13-9	14-0	14-3	14-6	14-8	14-11	15-2
	24.0	9-9	10-2	10-6	10-10	11-2	11-5	11-9	12-0	12-3	12-6	12-9	13-0	13-3	13-5	13-8	13-10	14-1
2 × 8	12.0	16-2	16-10	17-5	18-0	18-6	19-0	19-6	19-11	20-5	20-10	21-2	21-7	21-11	22-4	22-8	23-0	23-4
	16.0	14-8	15-3	15-10	16-4	16-10	17-3	17-9	18-1	18-6	18-11	19-3	19-7	19-11	20-3	20-7	20-11	21-2
	19.2	13-10	14-5	14-11	15-5	15-10	16-3	16-8	17-1	17-5	17-9	18-1	18-5	18-9	19-1	19-5	19-8	19-11
	24.0	12-10	13-4	13-10	14-3	14-8	15-1	15-6	15-10	16-2	16-6	16-10	17-2	17-5	17-9	18-0	18-3	18-6
2 × 10	12.0	20-8	21-6	22-3	22-11	23-8	24-3	24-10	25-5	26-0								
	16.0	18-9	19-6	20-2	20-10	21-6	22-1	22-7	23-1	23-8	24-1	24-7	25-0	25-5	25-10			
	19.2	17-8	18-4	19-0	19-7	20-2	20-9	21-3	21-9	22-3	22-8	23-1	23-7	23-11	24-4	24-9	25-1	25-5
	24.0	16-5	17-0	17-8	18-3	18-9	19-3	19-9	20-2	20-8	21-1	21-6	21-10	22-3	22-7	22-11	23-4	23-8
F_b	12.0	896	969	1,040	1,108	1,174	1,239	1,302	1,363	1,423	1,481	1,539	1,595	1,651	1,706	1,759	1,812	1,864
	16.0	986	1,067	1,145	1,220	1,293	1,364	1,433	1,500	1,566	1,631	1,694	1,756	1,817	1,877	1,936	1,995	2,052
	19.2	1,048	1,134	1,216	1,296	1,374	1,449	1,522	1,594	1,664	1,733	1,800	1,866	1,931	1,995	2,058	2,120	2,181
	24.0	1,129	1,221	1,310	1,396	1,480	1,561	1,640	1,717	1,793	1,866	1,939	2,010	2,080	2,149	2,217	2,283	2,349

NOTE: The required bending design value, F_b, in pounds per square inch (× 0.00689 for N/mm^2) is shown at the bottom of this table and is applicable to all lumber sizes shown. Spans are shown in feet-inches (1 foot = 304.8 mm, 1 inch = 25.4 mm) and are limited to 26 feet (7925 mm) and less.

TABLE 23-IV-R-1—RAFTERS WITH L/240 DEFLECTION LIMITATION

The allowable bending stress (F_b) and modulus of elasticity *(E)* used in this table shall be from Tables 23-IV-V-1 and 23-IV-V-2 only.

DESIGN CRITERIA:
Strength — Live load of 20 psf (0.96 kN/m^2) plus dead load of 10 psf (0.48 kN/m^2) determines the required bending design value.
Deflection — For 20 psf (0.96 kN/m^2) live load.
Limited to span in inches (mm) divided by 240.

Rafter Size (in)	Spacing (in)	Bending Design Value, F_b (psi) × 0.00689 for N/mm^2										
× 25.4 for mm		300	400	500	600	700	800	900	1000	1100	1200	1300
2 × 6	12.0	7-1	8-2	9-2	10-0	10-10	11-7	12-4	13-0	13-7	14-2	14-9
	16.0	6-2	7-1	7-11	8-8	9-5	10-0	10-8	11-3	11-9	12-4	12-10
	19.2	5-7	6-6	7-3	7-11	8-7	9-2	9-9	10-3	10-9	11-3	11-8
	24.0	5-0	5-10	6-6	7-1	7-8	8-2	8-8	9-2	9-7	10-0	10-5
2 × 8	12.0	9-4	10-10	12-1	13-3	14-4	15-3	16-3	17-1	17-11	18-9	19-6
	16.0	8-1	9-4	10-6	11-6	12-5	13-3	14-0	14-10	15-6	16-3	16-10
	19.2	7-5	8-7	9-7	10-6	11-4	12-1	12-10	13-6	14-2	14-10	15-5
	24.0	6-7	7-8	8-7	9-4	10-1	10-10	11-6	12-1	12-8	13-3	13-9
2 × 10	12.0	11-11	13-9	15-5	16-11	18-3	19-6	20-8	21-10	22-10	23-11	24-10
	16.0	10-4	11-11	13-4	14-8	15-10	16-11	17-11	18-11	19-10	20-8	21-6
	19.2	9-5	10-11	12-2	13-4	14-5	15-5	16-4	17-3	18-1	18-11	19-8
	24.0	8-5	9-9	10-11	11-11	12-11	13-9	14-8	15-5	16-2	16-11	17-7
2 × 12	12.0	14-6	16-9	18-9	20-6	22-2	23-9	25-2				
	16.0	12-7	14-6	16-3	17-9	19-3	20-6	21-9	23-0	24-1	25-2	
	19.2	11-6	13-3	14-10	16-3	17-6	18-9	19-11	21-0	22-0	23-0	23-11
	24.0	10-3	11-10	13-3	14-6	15-8	16-9	17-9	18-9	19-8	20-6	21-5
E	12.0	0.15	0.24	0.33	0.44	0.55	0.67	0.80	0.94	1.09	1.24	1.40
	16.0	0.13	0.21	0.29	0.38	0.48	0.58	0.70	0.82	0.94	1.07	1.21
	19.2	0.12	0.19	0.26	0.35	0.44	0.53	0.64	0.75	0.86	0.98	1.10
	24.0	0.11	0.17	0.24	0.31	0.39	0.48	0.57	0.67	0.77	0.88	0.99

Rafter Size (in)	Spacing (in)	Bending Design Value, F_b (psi) × 0.00689 for N/mm^2										
× 25.4 for mm		1400	1500	1600	1700	1800	1900	2000	2100	2200	2300	2400
2 × 6	12.0	15-4	15-11	16-5	16-11	17-5	17-10					
	16.0	13-3	13-9	14-2	14-8	15-1	15-6	15-11	16-3			
	19.2	12-2	12-7	13-0	13-4	13-9	14-2	14-6	14-10	15-2	15-7	
	24.0	10-10	11-3	11-7	11-11	12-4	12-8	13-0	13-3	13-7	13-11	14-2
2 × 8	12.0	20-3	20-11	21-7	22-3	22-11	23-7					
	16.0	17-6	18-1	18-9	19-4	19-10	20-5	20-11	21-5			
	19.2	16-0	16-7	17-1	17-7	18-1	18-7	19-1	19-7	20-0	20-6	
	24.0	14-4	14-10	15-3	15-9	16-3	16-8	17-1	17-6	17-11	18-4	18-9
2 × 10	12.0	25-10										
	16.0	22-4	23-1	23-11	24-7	25-4	26-0					
	19.2	20-5	21-1	21-10	22-6	23-1	23-9	24-5	25-0	25-7		
	24.0	18-3	18-11	19-6	20-1	20-8	21-3	21-10	22-4	22-10	23-5	23-11
2 × 12	12.0											
	16.0											
	19.2	24-10	25-8									
	24.0	22-2	23-0	23-9	24-5	25-2	25-10					
E	12.0	1.56	1.73	1.91	2.09	2.28	2.47					
	16.0	1.35	1.50	1.65	1.81	1.97	2.14	2.31	2.48			
	19.2	1.23	1.37	1.51	1.65	1.80	1.95	2.11	2.27	2.43	2.60	
	24.0	1.10	1.22	1.35	1.48	1.61	1.75	1.89	2.03	2.18	2.33	2.48

NOTE: The required modulus of elasticity, *E*, in 1,000,000 pounds per square inch (psi) (× 0.00689 for N/mm^2) is shown at the bottom of this table, is limited to 2.6 million psi (17 914 N/mm^2) and less, and is applicable to all lumber sizes shown. Spans are shown in feet-inches (1 foot = 304.8 mm, 1 inch = 25.4 mm) and are limited to 26 feet (7925 mm) and less.

TABLE 23-IV-R-2—RAFTERS WITH L/240 DEFLECTION LIMITATION

The allowable bending stress (F_b) and modulus of elasticity *(E)* used in this table shall be from Tables 23-IV-V-1 and 23-IV-V-2 only.

DESIGN CRITERIA:
Strength — Live load of 30 psf (1.44 kN/m^2) plus dead load of 10 psf (0.48 kN/m^2) determines the required bending design value.
Deflection — For 30 psf (1.44 kN/m^2) live load.
Limited to span in inches (mm) divided by 240.

Rafter Size (in)	Spacing (in)	Bending Design Value, F_b (psi) × 0.00689 for N/mm^2										
× 25.4 for mm		300	400	500	600	700	800	900	1000	1100	1200	1300
2 × 6	12.0	6-2	7-1	7-11	8-8	9-5	10-0	10-8	11-3	11-9	12-4	12-10
	16.0	5-4	6-2	6-10	7-6	8-2	8-8	9-3	9-9	10-2	10-8	11-1
	19.2	4-10	5-7	6-3	6-10	7-5	7-11	8-5	8-11	9-4	9-9	10-1
	24.0	4-4	5-0	5-7	6-2	6-8	7-1	7-6	7-11	8-4	8-8	9-1
2 × 8	12.0	8-1	9-4	10-6	11-6	12-5	13-3	14-0	14-10	15-6	16-3	16-10
	16.0	7-0	8-1	9-1	9-11	10-9	11-6	12-2	12-10	13-5	14-0	14-7
	19.2	6-5	7-5	8-3	9-1	9-9	10-6	11-1	11-8	12-3	12-10	13-4
	24.0	5-9	6-7	7-5	8-1	8-9	9-4	9-11	10-6	11-0	11-6	11-11
2 × 10	12.0	10-4	11-11	13-4	14-8	15-10	16-11	17-11	18-11	19-10	20-8	21-6
	16.0	8-11	10-4	11-7	12-8	13-8	14-8	15-6	16-4	17-2	17-11	18-8
	19.2	8-2	9-5	10-7	11-7	12-6	13-4	14-2	14-11	15-8	16-4	17-0
	24.0	7-4	8-5	9-5	10-4	11-2	11-11	12-8	13-4	14-0	14-8	15-3
2 × 12	12.0	12-7	14-6	16-3	17-9	19-3	20-6	21-9	23-0	24-1	25-2	
	16.0	10-11	12-7	14-1	15-5	16-8	17-9	18-10	19-11	20-10	21-9	22-8
	19.2	9-11	11-6	12-10	14-1	15-2	16-3	17-3	18-2	19-0	19-11	20-8
	24.0	8-11	10-3	11-6	12-7	13-7	14-6	15-5	16-3	17-0	17-9	18-6
E	12.0	0.15	0.23	0.32	0.43	0.54	0.66	0.78	0.92	1.06	1.21	1.36
	16.0	0.13	0.20	0.28	0.37	0.47	0.57	0.68	0.80	0.92	1.05	1.18
	19.2	0.12	0.18	0.26	0.34	0.43	0.52	0.62	0.73	0.84	0.95	1.08
	24.0	0.11	0.16	0.23	0.30	0.38	0.46	0.55	0.65	0.75	0.85	0.96

Rafter Size (in)	Spacing (in)	Bending Design Value, F_b (psi) × 0.00689 for N/mm^2										
× 25.4 for mm		1400	1500	1600	1700	1800	1900	2000	2100	2200	2300	2400
2 × 6	12.0	13-3	13-9	14-2	14-8	15-1	15-6	15-11				
	16.0	11-6	11-11	12-4	12-8	13-1	13-5	13-9	14-1	14-5		
	19.2	10-6	10-10	11-3	11-7	11-11	12-3	12-7	12-10	13-2	13-6	
	24.0	9-5	9-9	10-0	10-4	10-8	10-11	11-3	11-6	11-9	12-0	12-4
2 × 8	12.0	17-6	18-1	18-9	19-4	19-10	20-5	20-11				
	16.0	15-2	15-8	16-3	16-9	17-2	17-8	18-1	18-7	19-0		
	19.2	13-10	14-4	14-10	15-3	15-8	16-2	16-7	16-11	17-4	17-9	
	24.0	12-5	12-10	13-3	13-8	14-0	14-5	14-10	15-2	15-6	15-10	16-3
2 × 10	12.0	22-4	23-1	23-11	24-7	25-4	26-0					
	16.0	19-4	20-0	20-8	21-4	21-11	22-6	23-1	23-8	24-3		
	19.2	17-8	18-3	18-11	19-6	20-0	20-7	21-1	21-8	22-2	22-8	
	24.0	15-10	16-4	16-11	17-5	17-11	18-5	18-11	19-4	19-10	20-3	20-8
2 × 12	12.0											
	16.0	23-6	24-4	25-2	25-11							
	19.2	21-6	22-3	23-0	23-8	24-4	25-0	25-8				
	24.0	19-3	19-11	20-6	21-2	21-9	22-5	23-0	23-6	24-1	24-8	25-2
E	12.0	1.52	1.69	1.86	2.04	2.22	2.41	2.60				
	16.0	1.32	1.46	1.61	1.76	1.92	2.08	2.25	2.42	2.60		
	19.2	1.20	1.33	1.47	1.61	1.75	1.90	2.05	2.21	2.37	2.53	
	24.0	1.08	1.19	1.31	1.44	1.57	1.70	1.84	1.98	2.12	2.27	2.41

NOTE: The required modulus of elasticity, *E*, in 1,000,000 pounds per square inch (psi) (× 0.00689 for N/mm^2) is shown at the bottom of this table, is limited to 2.6 million psi (17 914 N/mm^2) and less, and is applicable to all lumber sizes shown. Spans are shown in feet-inches (1 foot = 304.8 mm, 1 inch = 25.4 mm) and are limited to 26 feet (7925 mm) and less.

TABLE 23-IV-R-3—RAFTERS WITH *L*/240 DEFLECTION LIMITATION

The allowable bending stress (F_b) and modulus of elasticity *(E)* used in this table shall be from Tables 23-IV-V-1 and 23-IV-V-2 only.

DESIGN CRITERIA:
Strength — Live load of 20 psf (0.96 kN/m^2) plus dead load of 15 psf (0.72 kN/m^2) determines the required bending design value.
Deflection — For 20 psf (0.96 kN/m^2) live load.
Limited to span in inches (mm) divided by 240.

Rafter Size (in)	Spacing (in)	Bending Design Value, F_b (psi) × 0.00689 for N/mm^2												
× 25.4 for mm		300	400	500	600	700	800	900	1000	1100	1200	1300	1400	1500
2 × 6	12.0	6-7	7-7	8-6	9-4	10-0	10-9	11-5	12-0	12-7	13-2	13-8	14-2	14-8
	16.0	5-8	6-7	7-4	8-1	8-8	9-4	9-10	10-5	10-11	11-5	11-10	12-4	12-9
	19.2	5-2	6-0	6-9	7-4	7-11	8-6	9-0	9-6	9-11	10-5	10-10	11-3	11-7
	24.0	4-8	5-4	6-0	6-7	7-1	7-7	8-1	8-6	8-11	9-4	9-8	10-0	10-5
2 × 8	12.0	8-8	10-0	11-2	12-3	13-3	14-2	15-0	15-10	16-7	17-4	18-0	18-9	19-5
	16.0	7-6	8-8	9-8	10-7	11-6	12-3	13-0	13-8	14-4	15-0	15-7	16-3	16-9
	19.2	6-10	7-11	8-10	9-8	10-6	11-2	11-10	12-6	13-1	13-8	14-3	14-10	15-4
	24.0	6-2	7-1	7-11	8-8	9-4	10-0	10-7	11-2	11-9	12-3	12-9	13-3	13-8
2 × 10	12.0	11-1	12-9	14-3	15-8	16-11	18-1	19-2	20-2	21-2	22-1	23-0	23-11	24-9
	16.0	9-7	11-1	12-4	13-6	14-8	15-8	16-7	17-6	18-4	19-2	19-11	20-8	21-5
	19.2	8-9	10-1	11-3	12-4	13-4	14-3	15-2	15-11	16-9	17-6	18-2	18-11	19-7
	24.0	7-10	9-0	10-1	11-1	11-11	12-9	13-6	14-3	15-0	15-8	16-3	16-11	17-6
2 × 12	12.0	13-5	15-6	17-4	19-0	20-6	21-11	23-3	24-7	25-9				
	16.0	11-8	13-5	15-0	16-6	17-9	19-0	20-2	21-3	22-4	23-3	24-3	25-2	26-0
	19.2	10-8	12-3	13-9	15-0	16-3	17-4	18-5	19-5	20-4	21-3	22-2	23-0	23-9
	24.0	9-6	11-0	12-3	13-5	14-6	15-6	16-6	17-4	18-2	19-0	19-10	20-6	21-3
E	12.0	0.12	0.19	0.26	0.35	0.44	0.54	0.64	0.75	0.86	0.98	1.11	1.24	1.37
	16.0	0.11	0.16	0.23	0.30	0.38	0.46	0.55	0.65	0.75	0.85	0.96	1.07	1.19
	19.2	0.10	0.15	0.21	0.27	0.35	0.42	0.51	0.59	0.68	0.78	0.88	0.98	1.09
	24.0	0.09	0.13	0.19	0.25	0.31	0.38	0.45	0.53	0.61	0.70	0.78	0.88	0.97

Rafter Size (in)	Spacing (in)	Bending Design Value, F_b (psi) × 0.00689 for N/mm^2											
× 25.4 for mm		1600	1700	1800	1900	2000	2100	2200	2300	2400	2500	2600	2700
2 × 6	12.0	15-2	15-8	16-1	16-7	17-0	17-5	17-10					
	16.0	13-2	13-7	13-11	14-4	14-8	15-1	15-5	15-9	16-1	16-5		
	19.2	12-0	12-4	12-9	13-1	13-5	13-9	14-1	14-5	14-8	15-0	15-4	
	24.0	10-9	11-1	11-5	11-8	12-0	12-4	12-7	12-10	13-2	13-5	13-8	13-11
2 × 8	12.0	20-0	20-8	21-3	21-10	22-4	22-11	23-6					
	16.0	17-4	17-10	18-5	18-11	19-5	19-10	20-4	20-9	21-3	21-8		
	19.2	15-10	16-4	16-9	17-3	17-8	18-1	18-7	19-0	19-5	19-9	20-2	
	24.0	14-2	14-7	15-0	15-5	15-10	16-3	16-7	17-0	17-4	17-8	18-0	18-5
2 × 10	12.0	25-6											
	16.0	22-1	22-10	23-5	24-1	24-9	25-4	25-11					
	19.2	20-2	20-10	21-5	22-0	22-7	23-1	23-8	24-2	24-9	25-3	25-9	
	24.0	18-1	18-7	19-2	19-8	20-2	20-8	21-2	21-8	22-1	22-7	23-0	23-5
2 × 12	12.0												
	16.0												
	19.2	24-7	25-4	26-0									
	24.0	21-11	22-8	23-3	23-11	24-7	25-2	25-9					
E	12.0	1.51	1.66	1.81	1.96	2.12	2.28	2.44					
	16.0	1.31	1.44	1.56	1.70	1.83	1.97	2.11	2.26	2.41	2.56		
	19.2	1.20	1.31	1.43	1.55	1.67	1.80	1.93	2.06	2.20	2.34	2.48	
	24.0	1.07	1.17	1.28	1.39	1.50	1.61	1.73	1.85	1.97	2.09	2.22	2.35

NOTE: The required modulus of elasticity, *E*, in 1,000,000 pounds per square inch (psi) (× 0.00689 for N/mm^2) is shown at the bottom of this table, is limited to 2.6 million psi (17 914 N/mm^2) and less, and is applicable to all lumber sizes shown. Spans are shown in feet-inches (1 foot = 304.8 mm, 1 inch = 25.4 mm) and are limited to 26 feet (7925 mm) and less.

TABLE 23-IV-R-4—RAFTERS WITH *L*/240 DEFLECTION LIMITATION

The allowable bending stress (F_b) and modulus of elasticity (*E*) used in this table shall be from Tables 23-IV-V-1 and 23-IV-V-2 only.

DESIGN CRITERIA:
Strength — Live load of 30 psf (1.44 kN/m^2) plus dead load of 15 psf (0.72 kN/m^2) determines the required bending design value.
Deflection — For 30 psf (1.44 kN/m^2) live load.
Limited to span in inches (mm) divided by 240.

Rafter Size (in)	Spacing (in)	Bending Design Value, F_b (psi) × 0.00689 for N/mm^2												
× 25.4 for mm		300	400	500	600	700	800	900	1000	1100	1200	1300	1400	1500
2 × 6	12.0	5-10	6-8	7-6	8-2	8-10	9-6	10-0	10-7	11-1	11-7	12-1	12-6	13-0
	16.0	5-0	5-10	6-6	7-1	7-8	8-2	8-8	9-2	9-7	10-0	10-5	10-10	11-3
	19.2	4-7	5-4	5-11	6-6	7-0	7-6	7-11	8-4	8-9	9-2	9-6	9-11	10-3
	24.0	4-1	4-9	5-4	5-10	6-3	6-8	7-1	7-6	7-10	8-2	8-6	8-10	9-2
2 × 8	12.0	7-8	8-10	9-10	10-10	11-8	12-6	13-3	13-11	14-8	15-3	15-11	16-6	17-1
	16.0	6-7	7-8	8-7	9-4	10-1	10-10	11-6	12-1	12-8	13-3	13-9	14-4	14-10
	19.2	6-0	7-0	7-10	8-7	9-3	9-10	10-6	11-0	11-7	12-1	12-7	13-1	13-6
	24.0	5-5	6-3	7-0	7-8	8-3	8-10	9-4	9-10	10-4	10-10	11-3	11-8	12-1
2 × 10	12.0	9-9	11-3	12-7	13-9	14-11	15-11	16-11	17-10	18-8	19-6	20-4	21-1	21-10
	16.0	8-5	9-9	10-11	11-11	12-11	13-9	14-8	15-5	16-2	16-11	17-7	18-3	18-11
	19.2	7-8	8-11	9-11	10-11	11-9	12-7	13-4	14-1	14-9	15-5	16-1	16-8	17-3
	24.0	6-11	8-0	8-11	9-9	10-6	11-3	11-11	12-7	13-2	13-9	14-4	14-11	15-5
2 × 12	12.0	11-10	13-8	15-4	16-9	18-1	19-4	20-6	21-8	22-8	23-9	24-8	25-7	
	16.0	10-3	11-10	13-3	14-6	15-8	16-9	17-9	18-9	19-8	20-6	21-5	22-2	23-0
	19.2	9-4	10-10	12-1	13-3	14-4	15-4	16-3	17-1	17-11	18-9	19-6	20-3	21-0
	24.0	8-5	9-8	10-10	11-10	12-10	13-8	14-6	15-4	16-1	16-9	17-5	18-1	18-9
E	12.0	0.13	0.19	0.27	0.36	0.45	0.55	0.66	0.77	0.89	1.01	1.14	1.28	1.41
	16.0	0.11	0.17	0.24	0.31	0.39	0.48	0.57	0.67	0.77	0.88	0.99	1.10	1.22
	19.2	0.10	0.15	0.22	0.28	0.36	0.44	0.52	0.61	0.70	0.80	0.90	1.01	1.12
	24.0	0.09	0.14	0.19	0.25	0.32	0.39	0.46	0.54	0.63	0.72	0.81	0.90	1.00

Rafter Size (in)	Spacing (in)	Bending Design Value, F_b (psi) × 0.00689 for N/mm^2											
× 25.4 for mm		1600	1700	1800	1900	2000	2100	2200	2300	2400	2500	2600	2700
2 × 6	12.0	13-5	13-10	14-2	14-7	15-0	15-4	15-8					
	16.0	11-7	11-11	12-4	12-8	13-0	13-3	13-7	13-11	14-2			
	19.2	10-7	10-11	11-3	11-6	11-10	12-2	12-5	12-8	13-0	13-3	13-6	
	24.0	9-6	9-9	10-0	10-4	10-7	10-10	11-1	11-4	11-7	11-10	12-1	12-4
2 × 8	12.0	17-8	18-2	18-9	19-3	19-9	20-3	20-8					
	16.0	15-3	15-9	16-3	16-8	17-1	17-6	17-11	18-4	18-9			
	19.2	13-11	14-5	14-10	15-2	15-7	16-0	16-4	16-9	17-1	17-5	17-9	
	24.0	12-6	12-10	13-3	13-7	13-11	14-4	14-8	15-0	15-3	15-7	15-11	16-3
2 × 10	12.0	22-6	23-3	23-11	24-6	25-2	25-10						
	16.0	19-6	20-1	20-8	21-3	21-10	22-4	22-10	23-5	23-11			
	19.2	17-10	18-4	18-11	19-5	19-11	20-5	20-10	21-4	21-10	22-3	22-8	
	24.0	15-11	16-5	16-11	17-4	17-10	18-3	18-8	19-1	19-6	19-11	20-4	20-8
2 × 12	12.0												
	16.0	23-9	24-5	25-2	25-10								
	19.2	21-8	22-4	23-0	23-7	24-2	24-10	25-5	25-11				
	24.0	19-4	20-0	20-6	21-1	21-8	22-2	22-8	23-3	23-9	24-2	24-8	25-2
E	12.0	1.56	1.71	1.86	2.02	2.18	2.34	2.51					
	16.0	1.35	1.48	1.61	1.75	1.89	2.03	2.18	2.33	2.48			
	19.2	1.23	1.35	1.47	1.59	1.72	1.85	1.99	2.12	2.26	2.41	2.55	
	24.0	1.10	1.21	1.31	1.43	1.54	1.66	1.78	1.90	2.02	2.15	2.28	2.41

NOTE: The required modulus of elasticity, *E*, in 1,000,000 pounds per square inch (psi) (× 0.00689 for N/mm^2) is shown at the bottom of this table, is limited to 2.6 million psi (17 914 N/mm^2) and less, and is applicable to all lumber sizes shown. Spans are shown in feet-inches (1 foot = 304.8 mm, 1 inch = 25.4 mm) and are limited to 26 feet (7925 mm) and less.

TABLE 23-IV-R-5—RAFTERS WITH *L*/240 DEFLECTION LIMITATION

The allowable bending stress (F_b) and modulus of elasticity *(E)* used in this table shall be from Tables 23-IV-V-1 and 23-IV-V-2 only.

DESIGN CRITERIA:
Strength — Live load of 20 psf (0.96 kN/m^2) plus dead load of 20 psf (0.96 kN/m^2) determines the required bending design value.
Deflection — For 20 psf (0.96 kN/m^2) live load.
Limited to span in inches (mm) divided by 240.

Rafter Size (in)	Spacing (in)	Bending Design Value, F_b (psi) × 0.00689 for N/mm^2												
× 25.4 for mm		300	400	500	600	700	800	900	1000	1100	1200	1300	1400	1500
2 × 6	12.0	6-2	7-1	7-11	8-8	9-5	10-0	10-8	11-3	11-9	12-4	12-10	13-3	13-9
	16.0	5-4	6-2	6-10	7-6	8-2	8-8	9-3	9-9	10-2	10-8	11-1	11-6	11-11
	19.2	4-10	5-7	6-3	6-10	7-5	7-11	8-5	8-11	9-4	9-9	10-1	10-6	10-10
	24.0	4-4	5-0	5-7	6-2	6-8	7-1	7-6	7-11	8-4	8-8	9-1	9-5	9-9
2 × 8	12.0	8-1	9-4	10-6	11-6	12-5	13-3	14-0	14-10	15-6	16-3	16-10	17-6	18-1
	16.0	7-0	8-1	9-1	9-11	10-9	11-6	12-2	12-10	13-5	14-0	14-7	15-2	15-8
	19.2	6-5	7-5	8-3	9-1	9-9	10-6	11-1	11-8	12-3	12-10	13-4	13-10	14-4
	24.0	5-9	6-7	7-5	8-1	8-9	9-4	9-11	10-6	11-0	11-6	11-11	12-5	12-10
2 × 10	12.0	10-4	11-11	13-4	14-8	15-10	16-11	17-11	18-11	19-10	20-8	21-6	22-4	23-1
	16.0	8-11	10-4	11-7	12-8	13-8	14-8	15-6	16-4	17-2	17-11	18-8	19-4	20-0
	19.2	8-2	9-5	10-7	11-7	12-6	13-4	14-2	14-11	15-8	16-4	17-0	17-8	18-3
	24.0	7-4	8-5	9-5	10-4	11-2	11-11	12-8	13-4	14-0	14-8	15-3	15-10	16-4
2 × 12	12.0	12-7	14-6	16-3	17-9	19-3	20-6	21-9	23-0	24-1	25-2			
	16.0	10-11	12-7	14-1	15-5	16-8	17-9	18-10	19-11	20-10	21-9	22-8	23-6	24-4
	19.2	9-11	11-6	12-10	14-1	15-2	16-3	17-3	18-2	19-0	19-11	20-8	21-6	22-3
	24.0	8-11	10-3	11-6	12-7	13-7	14-6	15-5	16-3	17-0	17-9	18-6	19-3	19-11
E	12.0	0.10	0.15	0.22	0.28	0.36	0.44	0.52	0.61	0.71	0.80	0.91	1.01	1.13
	16.0	0.09	0.13	0.19	0.25	0.31	0.38	0.45	0.53	0.61	0.70	0.79	0.88	0.97
	19.2	0.08	0.12	0.17	0.23	0.28	0.35	0.41	0.48	0.56	0.64	0.72	0.80	0.89
	24.0	0.07	0.11	0.15	0.20	0.25	0.31	0.37	0.43	0.50	0.57	0.64	0.72	0.80

Rafter Size (in)	Spacing (in)	Bending Design Value, F_b (psi) × 0.00689 for N/mm^2											
× 25.4 for mm		1600	1700	1800	1900	2000	2100	2200	2300	2400	2500	2600	2700
2 × 6	12.0	14-2	14-8	15-1	15-6	15-11	16-3	16-8	17-0	17-5	17-9	18-1	
	16.0	12-4	12-8	13-1	13-5	13-9	14-1	14-5	14-9	15-1	15-4	15-8	16-0
	19.2	11-3	11-7	11-11	12-3	12-7	12-10	13-2	13-6	13-9	14-0	14-4	14-7
	24.0	10-0	10-4	10-8	10-11	11-3	11-6	11-9	12-0	12-4	12-7	12-10	13-1
2 × 8	12.0	18-9	19-4	19-10	20-5	20-11	21-5	21-11	22-5	22-11	23-5	23-10	
	16.0	16-3	16-9	17-2	17-8	18-1	18-7	19-0	19-5	19-10	20-3	20-8	21-1
	19.2	14-10	15-3	15-8	16-2	16-7	16-11	17-4	17-9	18-1	18-6	18-10	19-3
	24.0	13-3	13-8	14-0	14-5	14-10	15-2	15-6	15-10	16-3	16-7	16-10	17-2
2 × 10	12.0	23-11	24-7	25-4	26-0								
	16.0	20-8	21-4	21-11	22-6	23-1	23-8	24-3	24-10	25-4	25-10		
	19.2	18-11	19-6	20-0	20-7	21-1	21-8	22-2	22-8	23-1	23-7	24-1	24-6
	24.0	16-11	17-5	17-11	18-5	18-11	19-4	19-10	20-3	20-8	21-1	21-6	21-11
2 × 12	12.0												
	16.0	25-2	25-11										
	19.2	23-0	23-8	24-4	25-0	25-8							
	24.0	20-6	21-2	21-9	22-5	23-0	23-6	24-1	24-8	25-2	25-8		
E	12.0	1.24	1.36	1.48	1.60	1.73	1.86	2.00	2.14	2.28	2.42	2.57	
	16.0	1.07	1.18	1.28	1.39	1.50	1.61	1.73	1.85	1.97	2.10	2.22	2.35
	19.2	0.98	1.07	1.17	1.27	1.37	1.47	1.58	1.69	1.80	1.91	2.03	2.15
	24.0	0.88	0.96	1.05	1.13	1.22	1.32	1.41	1.51	1.61	1.71	1.82	1.92

NOTE: The required modulus of elasticity, *E*, in 1,000,000 pounds per square inch (psi) (× 0.00689 for N/mm^2) is shown at the bottom of this table, is limited to 2.6 million psi (17 914 N/mm^2) and less, and is applicable to all lumber sizes shown. Spans are shown in feet-inches (1 foot = 304.8 mm, 1 inch = 25.4 mm) and are limited to 26 feet (7925 mm) and less.

TABLE 23-IV-R-6—RAFTERS WITH L/240 DEFLECTION LIMITATION

The allowable bending stress (F_b) and modulus of elasticity (*E*) used in this table shall be from Tables 23-IV-V-1 and 23-IV-V-2 only.

DESIGN CRITERIA:
Strength — Live load of 30 psf (1.44 kN/m²) plus dead load of 20 psf (0.96 kN/m²) determines the required bending design value.
Deflection — For 30 psf (1.44 kN/m²) live load.
Limited to span in inches (mm) divided by 240.

Rafter Size (in)	Spacing (in)	Bending Design Value, F_b (psi) × 0.00689 for N/mm²												
× 25.4 for mm		300	400	500	600	700	800	900	1000	1100	1200	1300	1400	1500
2 × 6	12.0	5-6	6-4	7-1	7-9	8-5	9-0	9-6	10-0	10-6	11-0	11-5	11-11	12-4
	16.0	4-9	5-6	6-2	6-9	7-3	7-9	8-3	8-8	9-1	9-6	9-11	10-3	10-8
	19.2	4-4	5-0	5-7	6-2	6-8	7-1	7-6	7-11	8-4	8-8	9-1	9-5	9-9
	24.0	3-11	4-6	5-0	5-6	5-11	6-4	6-9	7-1	7-5	7-9	8-1	8-5	8-8
2 × 8	12.0	7-3	8-4	9-4	10-3	11-1	11-10	12-7	13-3	13-11	14-6	15-1	15-8	16-3
	16.0	6-3	7-3	8-1	8-11	9-7	10-3	10-10	11-6	12-0	12-7	13-1	13-7	14-0
	19.2	5-9	6-7	7-5	8-1	8-9	9-4	9-11	10-6	11-0	11-6	11-11	12-5	12-10
	24.0	5-2	5-11	6-7	7-3	7-10	8-4	8-11	9-4	9-10	10-3	10-8	11-1	11-6
2 × 10	12.0	9-3	10-8	11-11	13-1	14-2	15-1	16-0	16-11	17-9	18-6	19-3	20-0	20-8
	16.0	8-0	9-3	10-4	11-4	12-3	13-1	13-10	14-8	15-4	16-0	16-8	17-4	17-11
	19.2	7-4	8-5	9-5	10-4	11-2	11-11	12-8	13-4	14-0	14-8	15-3	15-10	16-4
	24.0	6-6	7-7	8-5	9-3	10-0	10-8	11-4	11-11	12-6	13-1	13-7	14-2	14-8
2 × 12	12.0	11-3	13-0	14-6	15-11	17-2	18-4	19-6	20-6	21-7	22-6	23-5	24-4	25-2
	16.0	9-9	11-3	12-7	13-9	14-11	15-11	16-10	17-9	18-8	19-6	20-3	21-1	21-9
	19.2	8-11	10-3	11-6	12-7	13-7	14-6	15-5	16-3	17-0	17-9	18-6	19-3	19-11
	24.0	7-11	9-2	10-3	11-3	12-2	13-0	13-9	14-6	15-3	15-11	16-7	17-2	17-9
E	12.0	0.11	0.17	0.23	0.31	0.38	0.47	0.56	0.66	0.76	0.86	0.97	1.09	1.21
	16.0	0.09	0.14	0.20	0.26	0.33	0.41	0.49	0.57	0.66	0.75	0.84	0.94	1.05
	19.2	0.09	0.13	0.18	0.24	0.30	0.37	0.44	0.52	0.60	0.68	0.77	0.86	0.95
	24.0	0.08	0.12	0.16	0.22	0.27	0.33	0.40	0.46	0.54	0.61	0.69	0.77	0.85

Rafter Size (in)	Spacing (in)	Bending Design Value, F_b (psi) × 0.00689 for N/mm²											
× 25.4 for mm		1600	1700	1800	1900	2000	2100	2200	2300	2400	2500	2600	2700
2 × 6	12.0	12-8	13-1	13-6	13-10	14-2	14-7	14-11	15-3	15-7	15-11		
	16.0	11-0	11-4	11-8	12-0	12-4	12-7	12-11	13-2	13-6	13-9	14-0	14-3
	19.2	10-0	10-4	10-8	10-11	11-3	11-6	11-9	12-0	12-4	12-7	12-10	13-1
	24.0	9-0	9-3	9-6	9-9	10-0	10-3	10-6	10-9	11-0	11-3	11-5	11-8
2 × 8	12.0	16-9	17-3	17-9	18-3	18-9	19-2	19-8	20-1	20-6	20-11		
	16.0	14-6	14-11	15-5	15-10	16-3	16-7	17-0	17-5	17-9	18-1	18-6	18-10
	19.2	13-3	13-8	14-0	14-5	14-10	15-2	15-6	15-10	16-3	16-7	16-10	17-2
	24.0	11-10	12-2	12-7	12-11	13-3	13-7	13-11	14-2	14-6	14-10	15-1	15-5
2 × 10	12.0	21-4	22-0	22-8	23-3	23-11	24-6	25-1	25-7				
	16.0	18-6	19-1	19-7	20-2	20-8	21-2	21-8	22-2	22-8	23-1	23-7	24-0
	19.2	16-11	17-5	17-11	18-5	18-11	19-4	19-10	20-3	20-8	21-1	21-6	21-11
	24.0	15-1	15-7	16-0	16-6	16-11	17-4	17-9	18-1	18-6	18-11	19-3	19-7
2 × 12	12.0	26-0											
	16.0	22-6	23-2	23-10	24-6	25-2	25-9						
	19.2	20-6	21-2	21-9	22-5	23-0	23-6	24-1	24-8	25-2	25-8		
	24.0	18-4	18-11	19-6	20-0	20-6	21-1	21-7	22-0	22-6	23-0	23-5	23-10
E	12.0	1.33	1.46	1.59	1.72	1.86	2.00	2.14	2.29	2.44	2.60		
	16.0	1.15	1.26	1.37	1.49	1.61	1.73	1.86	1.99	2.12	2.25	2.39	2.53
	19.2	1.05	1.15	1.25	1.36	1.47	1.58	1.70	1.81	1.93	2.05	2.18	2.31
	24.0	0.94	1.03	1.12	1.22	1.31	1.41	1.52	1.62	1.73	1.84	1.95	2.06

NOTE: The required modulus of elasticity, *E*, in 1,000,000 pounds per square inch (psi) (× 0.00689 for N/mm²) is shown at the bottom of this table, is limited to 2.6 million psi (17 914 N/mm²) and less, and is applicable to all lumber sizes shown. Spans are shown in feet-inches (1 foot = 304.8 mm, 1 inch = 25.4 mm) and are limited to 26 feet (7925 mm) and less.

TABLE 23-IV-R-7—RAFTERS WITH *L*/180 DEFLECTION LIMITATION

The allowable bending stress (F_b) and modulus of elasticity *(E)* used in this table shall be from Tables 23-IV-V-1 and 23-IV-V-2 only.

DESIGN CRITERIA:
Strength — Live load of 20 psf (0.96 kN/m^2) plus dead load of 10 psf (0.48 kN/m^2) determines the required bending design value.
Deflection — For 20 psf (0.96 kN/m^2) live load.
Limited to span in inches (mm) divided by 180.

Rafter Size (in)	Spacing (in)	Bending Design Value, F_b (psi) × 0.00689 for N/mm^2														
× 25.4 for mm		200	300	400	500	600	700	800	900	1000	1100	1200	1300	1400	1500	1600
2 × 4	12.0	3-8	4-6	5-3	5-10	6-5	6-11	7-5	7-10	8-3	8-8	9-0	9-5	9-9	10-1	10-5
	16.0	3-2	3-11	4-6	5-1	5-6	6-0	6-5	6-9	7-2	7-6	7-10	8-2	8-5	8-9	9-0
	19.2	2-11	3-7	4-1	4-7	5-1	5-5	5-10	6-2	6-6	6-10	7-2	7-5	7-9	8-0	8-3
	24.0	2-7	3-2	3-8	4-1	4-6	4-11	5-3	5-6	5-10	6-1	6-5	6-8	6-11	7-2	7-5
2 × 6	12.0	5-10	7-1	8-2	9-2	10-0	10-10	11-7	12-4	13-0	13-7	14-2	14-9	15-4	15-11	16-5
	16.0	5-0	6-2	7-1	7-11	8-8	9-5	10-0	10-8	11-3	11-9	12-4	12-10	13-3	13-9	14-2
	19.2	4-7	5-7	6-6	7-3	7-11	8-7	9-2	9-9	10-3	10-9	11-3	11-8	12-2	12-7	13-0
	24.0	4-1	5-0	5-10	6-6	7-1	7-8	8-2	8-8	9-2	9-7	10-0	10-5	10-10	11-3	11-7
2 × 8	12.0	7-8	9-4	10-10	12-1	13-3	14-4	15-3	16-3	17-1	17-11	18-9	19-6	20-3	20-11	21-7
	16.0	6-7	8-1	9-4	10-6	11-6	12-5	13-3	14-0	14-10	15-6	16-3	16-10	17-6	18-1	18-9
	19.2	6-0	7-5	8-7	9-7	10-6	11-4	12-1	12-10	13-6	14-2	14-10	15-5	16-0	16-7	17-1
	24.0	5-5	6-7	7-8	8-7	9-4	10-1	10-10	11-6	12-1	12-8	13-3	13-9	14-4	14-10	15-3
2 × 10	12.0	9-9	11-11	13-9	15-5	16-11	18-3	19-6	20-8	21-10	22-10	23-11	24-10	25-10		
	16.0	8-5	10-4	11-11	13-4	14-8	15-10	16-11	17-11	18-11	19-10	20-8	21-6	22-4	23-1	23-11
	19.2	7-8	9-5	10-11	12-2	13-4	14-5	15-5	16-4	17-3	18-1	18-11	19-8	20-5	21-1	21-10
	24.0	6-11	8-5	9-9	10-11	11-11	12-11	13-9	14-8	15-5	16-2	16-11	17-7	18-3	18-11	19-6
E	12.0	0.06	0.12	0.18	0.25	0.33	0.41	0.51	0.60	0.71	0.82	0.93	1.05	1.17	1.30	1.43
	16.0	0.05	0.10	0.15	0.22	0.28	0.36	0.44	0.52	0.61	0.71	0.80	0.91	1.01	1.13	1.24
	19.2	0.05	0.09	0.14	0.20	0.26	0.33	0.40	0.48	0.56	0.64	0.73	0.83	0.93	1.03	1.13
	24.0	0.04	0.08	0.13	0.18	0.23	0.29	0.36	0.43	0.50	0.58	0.66	0.74	0.83	0.92	1.01

Rafter Size (in)	Spacing (in)	Bending Design Value, F_b (psi) × 0.00689 for N/mm^2													
× 25.4 for mm		1700	1800	1900	2000	2100	2200	2300	2400	2500	2600	2700	2800	2900	3000
2 × 4	12.0	10-9	11-1	11-4	11-8	11-11	12-3	12-6							
	16.0	9-4	9-7	9-10	10-1	10-4	10-7	10-10	11-1	11-4	11-6				
	19.2	8-6	8-9	9-0	9-3	9-5	9-8	9-11	10-1	10-4	10-6	10-9			
	24.0	7-7	7-10	8-0	8-3	8-5	8-8	8-10	9-0	9-3	9-5	9-7	9-9	9-11	10-1
2 × 6	12.0	16-11	17-5	17-10	18-4	18-9	19-3	19-8							
	16.0	14-8	15-1	15-6	15-11	16-3	16-8	17-0	17-5	17-9	18-1				
	19.2	13-4	13-9	14-2	14-6	14-10	15-2	15-7	15-11	16-2	16-6	16-10			
	24.0	11-11	12-4	12-8	13-0	13-3	13-7	13-11	14-2	14-6	14-9	15-1	15-4	15-7	15-11
2 × 8	12.0	22-3	22-11	23-7	24-2	24-9	25-4	25-11							
	16.0	19-4	19-10	20-5	20-11	21-5	21-11	22-5	22-11	23-5	23-10				
	19.2	17-7	18-1	18-7	19-1	19-7	20-0	20-6	20-11	21-4	21-9	22-2			
	24.0	15-9	16-3	16-8	17-1	17-6	17-11	18-4	18-9	19-1	19-6	19-10	20-3	20-7	20-11
2 × 10	12.0														
	16.0	24-7	25-4	26-0											
	19.2	22-6	23-1	23-9	24-5	25-0	25-7								
	24.0	20-1	20-8	21-3	21-10	22-4	22-10	23-5	23-11	24-5	24-10	25-4	25-10		
E	12.0	1.57	1.71	1.85	2.00	2.15	2.31	2.47							
	16.0	1.36	1.48	1.60	1.73	1.86	2.00	2.14	2.28	2.42	2.57				
	19.2	1.24	1.35	1.46	1.58	1.70	1.82	1.95	2.08	2.21	2.34	2.48			
	24.0	1.11	1.21	1.31	1.41	1.52	1.63	1.74	1.86	1.98	2.10	2.22	2.34	2.47	2.60

NOTE: The required modulus of elasticity, *E*, in 1,000,000 pounds per square inch (psi) (× 0.00689 for N/mm^2) is shown at the bottom of this table, is limited to 2.6 million psi (17 914 N/mm^2) and less, and is applicable to all lumber sizes shown. Spans are shown in feet-inches (1 foot = 304.8 mm, 1 inch = 25.4 mm) and are limited to 26 feet (7925 mm) and less.

TABLE 23-IV-R-8—RAFTERS WITH *L*/180 DEFLECTION LIMITATION

The allowable bending stress (F_b) and modulus of elasticity *(E)* used in this table shall be from Tables 23-IV-V-1 and 23-IV-V-2 only.

DESIGN CRITERIA:
Strength — Live load of 30 psf (1.44 kN/m^2) plus dead load of 10 psf (0.48 kN/m^2) determines the required bending design value.
Deflection — For 30 psf (1.44 kN/m^2) live load.
Limited to span in inches (mm) divided by 180.

Rafter Size (in)	Spacing (in)	Bending Design Value, F_b (psi) × 0.00689 for N/mm^2														
× 25.4 for mm		200	300	400	500	600	700	800	900	1000	1100	1200	1300	1400	1500	1600
2 × 4	12.0	3-2	3-11	4-6	5-1	5-6	6-0	6-5	6-9	7-2	7-6	7-10	8-2	8-5	8-9	9-0
	16.0	2-9	3-5	3-11	4-4	4-10	5-2	5-6	5-10	6-2	6-6	6-9	7-1	7-4	7-7	7-10
	19.2	2-6	3-1	3-7	4-0	4-4	4-9	5-1	5-4	5-8	5-11	6-2	6-5	6-8	6-11	7-2
	24.0	2-3	2-9	3-2	3-7	3-11	4-3	4-6	4-10	5-1	5-4	5-6	5-9	6-0	6-2	6-5
2 × 6	12.0	5-0	6-2	7-1	7-11	8-8	9-5	10-0	10-8	11-3	11-9	12-4	12-10	13-3	13-9	14-2
	16.0	4-4	5-4	6-2	6-10	7-6	8-2	8-8	9-3	9-9	10-2	10-8	11-1	11-6	11-11	12-4
	19.2	4-0	4-10	5-7	6-3	6-10	7-5	7-11	8-5	8-11	9-4	9-9	10-1	10-6	10-10	11-3
	24.0	3-7	4-4	5-0	5-7	6-2	6-8	7-1	7-6	7-11	8-4	8-8	9-1	9-5	9-9	10-0
2 × 8	12.0	6-7	8-1	9-4	10-6	11-6	12-5	13-3	14-0	14-10	15-6	16-3	16-10	17-6	18-1	18-9
	16.0	5-9	7-0	8-1	9-1	9-11	10-9	11-6	12-2	12-10	13-5	14-0	14-7	15-2	15-8	16-3
	19.2	5-3	6-5	7-5	8-3	9-1	9-9	10-6	11-1	11-8	12-3	12-10	13-4	13-10	14-4	14-10
	24.0	4-8	5-9	6-7	7-5	8-1	8-9	9-4	9-11	10-6	11-0	11-6	11-11	12-5	12-10	13-3
2 × 10	12.0	8-5	10-4	11-11	13-4	14-8	15-10	16-11	17-11	18-11	19-10	20-8	21-6	22-4	23-1	23-11
	16.0	7-4	8-11	10-4	11-7	12-8	13-8	14-8	15-6	16-4	17-2	17-11	18-8	19-4	20-0	20-8
	19.2	6-8	8-2	9-5	10-7	11-7	12-6	13-4	14-2	14-11	15-8	16-4	17-0	17-8	18-3	18-11
	24.0	6-0	7-4	8-5	9-5	10-4	11-2	11-11	12-8	13-4	14-0	14-8	15-3	15-10	16-4	16-11
E	12.0	0.06	0.11	0.17	0.24	0.32	0.40	0.49	0.59	0.69	0.79	0.91	1.02	1.14	1.27	1.39
	16.0	0.05	0.10	0.15	0.21	0.28	0.35	0.43	0.51	0.60	0.69	0.78	0.88	0.99	1.10	1.21
	19.2	0.05	0.09	0.14	0.19	0.25	0.32	0.39	0.47	0.54	0.63	0.72	0.81	0.90	1.00	1.10
	24.0	0.04	0.08	0.12	0.17	0.23	0.29	0.35	0.42	0.49	0.56	0.64	0.72	0.81	0.89	0.99

Rafter Size (in)	Spacing (in)	Bending Design Value, F_b (psi) × 0.00689 for N/mm^2													
× 25.4 for mm		1700	1800	1900	2000	2100	2200	2300	2400	2500	2600	2700	2800	2900	3000
2 × 4	12.0	9-4	9-7	9-10	10-1	10-4	10-7	10-10	11-1						
	16.0	8-1	8-4	8-6	8-9	9-0	9-2	9-5	9-7	9-9	10-0				
	19.2	7-4	7-7	7-9	8-0	8-2	8-5	8-7	8-9	8-11	9-1	9-3	9-5		
	24.0	6-7	6-9	7-0	7-2	7-4	7-6	7-8	7-10	8-0	8-2	8-4	8-5	8-7	8-9
2 × 6	12.0	14-8	15-1	15-6	15-11	16-3	16-8	17-0	17-5						
	16.0	12-8	13-1	13-5	13-9	14-1	14-5	14-9	15-1	15-4	15-8				
	19.2	11-7	11-11	12-3	12-7	12-10	13-2	13-6	13-9	14-0	14-4	14-7	14-10		
	24.0	10-4	10-8	10-11	11-3	11-6	11-9	12-0	12-4	12-7	12-10	13-1	13-3	13-6	13-9
2 × 8	12.0	19-4	19-10	20-5	20-11	21-5	21-11	22-5	22-11						
	16.0	16-9	17-2	17-8	18-1	18-7	19-0	19-5	19-10	20-3	20-8				
	19.2	15-3	15-8	16-2	16-7	16-11	17-4	17-9	18-1	18-6	18-10	19-3	19-7		
	24.0	13-8	14-0	14-5	14-10	15-2	15-6	15-10	16-3	16-7	16-10	17-2	17-6	17-10	18-1
2 × 10	12.0	24-7	25-4	26-0											
	16.0	21-4	21-11	22-6	23-1	23-8	24-3	24-10	25-4	25-10					
	19.2	19-6	20-0	20-7	21-1	21-8	22-2	22-8	23-1	23-7	24-1	24-6	25-0		
	24.0	17-5	17-11	18-5	18-11	19-4	19-10	20-3	20-8	21-1	21-6	21-11	22-4	22-9	23-1
E	12.0	1.53	1.66	1.80	1.95	2.10	2.25	2.40	2.56						
	16.0	1.32	1.44	1.56	1.69	1.82	1.95	2.08	2.22	2.36	2.50				
	19.2	1.21	1.32	1.43	1.54	1.66	1.78	1.90	2.03	2.15	2.28	2.42	2.55		
	24.0	1.08	1.18	1.28	1.38	1.48	1.59	1.70	1.81	1.93	2.04	2.16	2.28	2.41	2.53

NOTE: The required modulus of elasticity, *E*, in 1,000,000 pounds per square inch (psi) (× 0.00689 for N/mm^2) is shown at the bottom of this table, is limited to 2.6 million psi (17 914 N/mm^2) and less, and is applicable to all lumber sizes shown. Spans are shown in feet-inches (1 foot = 304.8 mm, 1 inch = 25.4 mm) and are limited to 26 feet (7925 mm) and less.

TABLE 23-IV-R-9—RAFTERS WITH *L*/180 DEFLECTION LIMITATION

The allowable bending stress (F_b) and modulus of elasticity *(E)* used in this table shall be from Tables 23-IV-V-1 and 23-IV-V-2 only.

DESIGN CRITERIA:
Strength — Live load of 20 psf (0.96 kN/m^2) plus dead load of 15 psf (0.72 kN/m^2) determines the required bending design value.
Deflection — For 20 psf (0.96 kN/m^2) live load.
Limited to span in inches (mm) divided by 180.

Rafter Size (in)	Spacing (in)	Bending Design Value, F_b (psi) × 0.00689 for N/mm^2														
× 25.4 for mm		200	300	400	500	600	700	800	900	1000	1100	1200	1300	1400	1500	1600
2 × 4	12.0	3-5	4-2	4-10	5-5	5-11	6-5	6-10	7-3	7-8	8-0	8-4	8-8	9-0	9-4	9-8
	16.0	2-11	3-7	4-2	4-8	5-1	5-6	5-11	6-3	6-7	6-11	7-3	7-6	7-10	8-1	8-4
	19.2	2-8	3-4	3-10	4-3	4-8	5-1	5-5	5-9	6-0	6-4	6-7	6-11	7-2	7-5	7-8
	24.0	2-5	2-11	3-5	3-10	4-2	4-6	4-10	5-1	5-5	5-8	5-11	6-2	6-5	6-7	6-10
2 × 6	12.0	5-4	6-7	7-7	8-6	9-4	10-0	10-9	11-5	12-0	12-7	13-2	13-8	14-2	14-8	15-2
	16.0	4-8	5-8	6-7	7-4	8-1	8-8	9-4	9-10	10-5	10-11	11-5	11-10	12-4	12-9	13-2
	19.2	4-3	5-2	6-0	6-9	7-4	7-11	8-6	9-0	9-6	9-11	10-5	10-10	11-3	11-7	12-0
	24.0	3-10	4-8	5-4	6-0	6-7	7-1	7-7	8-1	8-6	8-11	9-4	9-8	10-0	10-5	10-9
2 × 8	12.0	7-1	8-8	10-0	11-2	12-3	13-3	14-2	15-0	15-10	16-7	17-4	18-0	18-9	19-5	20-0
	16.0	6-2	7-6	8-8	9-8	10-7	11-6	12-3	13-0	13-8	14-4	15-0	15-7	16-3	16-9	17-4
	19.2	5-7	6-10	7-11	8-10	9-8	10-6	11-2	11-10	12-6	13-1	13-8	14-3	14-10	15-4	15-10
	24.0	5-0	6-2	7-1	7-11	8-8	9-4	10-0	10-7	11-2	11-9	12-3	12-9	13-3	13-8	14-2
2 × 10	12.0	9-0	11-1	12-9	14-3	15-8	16-11	18-1	19-2	20-2	21-2	22-1	23-0	23-11	24-9	25-6
	16.0	7-10	9-7	11-1	12-4	13-6	14-8	15-8	16-7	17-6	18-4	19-2	19-11	20-8	21-5	22-1
	19.2	7-2	8-9	10-1	11-3	12-4	13-4	14-3	15-2	15-11	16-9	17-6	18-2	18-11	19-7	20-2
	24.0	6-5	7-10	9-0	10-1	11-1	11-11	12-9	13-6	14-3	15-0	15-8	16-3	16-11	17-6	18-1
E	12.0	0.05	0.09	0.14	0.20	0.26	0.33	0.40	0.48	0.56	0.65	0.74	0.83	0.93	1.03	1.14
	16.0	0.04	0.08	0.12	0.17	0.23	0.28	0.35	0.41	0.49	0.56	0.64	0.72	0.80	0.89	0.98
	19.2	0.04	0.07	0.11	0.16	0.21	0.26	0.32	0.38	0.44	0.51	0.58	0.66	0.73	0.81	0.90
	24.0	0.04	0.07	0.10	0.14	0.18	0.23	0.28	0.34	0.40	0.46	0.52	0.59	0.66	0.73	0.80

Rafter Size (in)	Spacing (in)	Bending Design Value, F_b (psi) × 0.00689 for N/mm^2													
× 25.4 for mm		1700	1800	1900	2000	2100	2200	2300	2400	2500	2600	2700	2800	2900	3000
2 × 4	12.0	9-11	10-3	10-6	10-10	11-1	11-4	11-7	11-10	12-1	12-4	12-7			
	16.0	8-7	8-10	9-1	9-4	9-7	9-10	10-0	10-3	10-5	10-8	10-10	11-1	11-3	11-5
	19.2	7-10	8-1	8-4	8-6	8-9	8-11	9-2	9-4	9-7	9-9	9-11	10-1	10-3	10-5
	24.0	7-0	7-3	7-5	7-8	7-10	8-0	8-2	8-4	8-6	8-8	8-10	9-0	9-2	9-4
2 × 6	12.0	15-8	16-1	16-7	17-0	17-5	17-10	18-2	18-7	19-0	19-4	19-9			
	16.0	13-7	13-11	14-4	14-8	15-1	15-5	15-9	16-1	16-5	16-9	17-1	17-5	17-8	18-0
	19.2	12-4	12-9	13-1	13-5	13-9	14-1	14-5	14-8	15-0	15-4	15-7	15-11	16-2	16-5
	24.0	11-1	11-5	11-8	12-0	12-4	12-7	12-10	13-2	13-5	13-8	13-11	14-2	14-5	14-8
2 × 8	12.0	20-8	21-3	21-10	22-4	22-11	23-6	24-0	24-6	25-0	25-6	26-0			
	16.0	17-10	18-5	18-11	19-5	19-10	20-4	20-9	21-3	21-8	22-1	22-6	22-11	23-4	23-9
	19.2	16-4	16-9	17-3	17-8	18-1	18-7	19-0	19-5	19-9	20-2	20-7	20-11	21-4	21-8
	24.0	14-7	15-0	15-5	15-10	16-3	16-7	17-0	17-4	17-8	18-0	18-5	18-9	19-1	19-5
2 × 10	12.0														
	16.0	22-10	23-5	24-1	24-9	25-4	25-11								
	19.2	20-10	21-5	22-0	22-7	23-1	23-8	24-2	24-9	25-3	25-9				
	24.0	18-7	19-2	19-8	20-2	20-8	21-2	21-8	22-1	22-7	23-0	23-5	23-11	24-4	24-9
E	12.0	1.24	1.36	1.47	1.59	1.71	1.83	1.96	2.09	2.22	2.35	2.49			
	16.0	1.08	1.17	1.27	1.37	1.48	1.59	1.70	1.81	1.92	2.04	2.16	2.28	2.40	2.53
	19.2	0.98	1.07	1.16	1.25	1.35	1.45	1.55	1.65	1.75	1.86	1.97	2.08	2.19	2.31
	24.0	0.88	0.96	1.04	1.12	1.21	1.29	1.38	1.48	1.57	1.66	1.76	1.86	1.96	2.06

NOTE: The required modulus of elasticity, *E*, in 1,000,000 pounds per square inch (psi) (× 0.00689 for N/mm^2) is shown at the bottom of this table, is limited to 2.6 million psi (17 914 N/mm^2) and less, and is applicable to all lumber sizes shown. Spans are shown in feet-inches (1 foot = 304.8 mm, 1 inch = 25.4 mm) and are limited to 26 feet (7925 mm) and less.

TABLE 23-IV-R-10—RAFTERS WITH *L*/180 DEFLECTION LIMITATION

The allowable bending stress (F_b) and modulus of elasticity *(E)* used in this table shall be from Tables 23-IV-V-1 and 23-IV-V-2 only.

DESIGN CRITERIA:
Strength — Live load of 30 psf (1.44 kN/m^2) plus dead load of 15 psf (0.72 kN/m^2) determines the required bending design value.
Deflection — For 30 psf (1.44 kN/m^2) live load.
Limited to span in inches (mm) divided by 180.

Rafter Size (in)	Spacing (in)	Bending Design Value, F_b (psi) × 0.00689 for N/mm^2														
× 25.4 for mm		200	300	400	500	600	700	800	900	1000	1100	1200	1300	1400	1500	1600
2 × 4	12.0	3-0	3-8	4-3	4-9	5-3	5-8	6-0	6-5	6-9	7-1	7-5	7-8	8-0	8-3	8-6
	16.0	2-7	3-2	3-8	4-1	4-6	4-11	5-3	5-6	5-10	6-1	6-5	6-8	6-11	7-2	7-5
	19.2	2-5	2-11	3-4	3-9	4-1	4-5	4-9	5-1	5-4	5-7	5-10	6-1	6-4	6-6	6-9
	24.0	2-2	2-7	3-0	3-4	3-8	4-0	4-3	4-6	4-9	5-0	5-3	5-5	5-8	5-10	6-0
2 × 6	12.0	4-9	5-10	6-8	7-6	8-2	8-10	9-6	10-0	10-7	11-1	11-7	12-1	12-6	13-0	13-5
	16.0	4-1	5-0	5-10	6-6	7-1	7-8	8-2	8-8	9-2	9-7	10-0	10-5	10-10	11-3	11-7
	19.2	3-9	4-7	5-4	5-11	6-6	7-0	7-6	7-11	8-4	8-9	9-2	9-6	9-11	10-3	10-7
	24.0	3-4	4-1	4-9	5-4	5-10	6-3	6-8	7-1	7-6	7-10	8-2	8-6	8-10	9-2	9-6
2 × 8	12.0	6-3	7-8	8-10	9-10	10-10	11-8	12-6	13-3	13-11	14-8	15-3	15-11	16-6	17-1	17-8
	16.0	5-5	6-7	7-8	8-7	9-4	10-1	10-10	11-6	12-1	12-8	13-3	13-9	14-4	14-10	15-3
	19.2	4-11	6-0	7-0	7-10	8-7	9-3	9-10	10-6	11-0	11-7	12-1	12-7	13-1	13-6	13-11
	24.0	4-5	5-5	6-3	7-0	7-8	8-3	8-10	9-4	9-10	10-4	10-10	11-3	11-8	12-1	12-6
2 × 10	12.0	8-0	9-9	11-3	12-7	13-9	14-11	15-11	16-11	17-10	18-8	19-6	20-4	21-1	21-10	22-6
	16.0	6-11	8-5	9-9	10-11	11-11	12-11	13-9	14-8	15-5	16-2	16-11	17-7	18-3	18-11	19-6
	19.2	6-4	7-8	8-11	9-11	10-11	11-9	12-7	13-4	14-1	14-9	15-5	16-1	16-8	17-3	17-10
	24.0	5-8	6-11	8-0	8-11	9-9	10-6	11-3	11-11	12-7	13-2	13-9	14-4	14-11	15-5	15-11
E	12.0	0.05	0.09	0.15	0.20	0.27	0.34	0.41	0.49	0.58	0.67	0.76	0.86	0.96	1.06	1.17
	16.0	0.04	0.08	0.13	0.18	0.23	0.29	0.36	0.43	0.50	0.58	0.66	0.74	0.83	0.92	1.01
	19.2	0.04	0.08	0.12	0.16	0.21	0.27	0.33	0.39	0.46	0.53	0.60	0.68	0.76	0.84	0.92
	24.0	0.04	0.07	0.10	0.14	0.19	0.24	0.29	0.35	0.41	0.47	0.54	0.61	0.68	0.75	0.83

Rafter Size (in)	Spacing (in)	Bending Design Value, F_b (psi) × 0.00689 for N/mm^2													
× 25.4 for mm		1700	1800	1900	2000	2100	2200	2300	2400	2500	2600	2700	2800	2900	3000
2 × 4	12.0	8-9	9-0	9-3	9-6	9-9	10-0	10-3	10-5	10-8	10-10	11-1			
	16.0	7-7	7-10	8-0	8-3	8-5	8-8	8-10	9-0	9-3	9-5	9-7	9-9	9-11	10-1
	19.2	6-11	7-2	7-4	7-6	7-9	7-11	8-1	8-3	8-5	8-7	8-9	8-11	9-1	9-3
	24.0	6-3	6-5	6-7	6-9	6-11	7-1	7-3	7-5	7-6	7-8	7-10	8-0	8-1	8-3
2 × 6	12.0	13-10	14-2	14-7	15-0	15-4	15-8	16-1	16-5	16-9	17-1	17-5			
	16.0	11-11	12-4	12-8	13-0	13-3	13-7	13-11	14-2	14-6	14-9	15-1	15-4	15-7	15-11
	19.2	10-11	11-3	11-6	11-10	12-2	12-5	12-8	13-0	13-3	13-6	13-9	14-0	14-3	14-6
	24.0	9-9	10-0	10-4	10-7	10-10	11-1	11-4	11-7	11-10	12-1	12-4	12-6	12-9	13-0
2 × 8	12.0	18-2	18-9	19-3	19-9	20-3	20-8	21-2	21-7	22-1	22-6	22-11			
	16.0	15-9	16-3	16-8	17-1	17-6	17-11	18-4	18-9	19-1	19-6	19-10	20-3	20-7	20-11
	19.2	14-5	14-10	15-2	15-7	16-0	16-4	16-9	17-1	17-5	17-9	18-1	18-5	18-9	19-1
	24.0	12-10	13-3	13-7	13-11	14-4	14-8	15-0	15-3	15-7	15-11	16-3	16-6	16-10	17-1
2 × 10	12.0	23-3	23-11	24-6	25-2	25-10									
	16.0	20-1	20-8	21-3	21-10	22-4	22-10	23-5	23-11	24-5	24-10	25-4	25-10		
	19.2	18-4	18-11	19-5	19-11	20-5	20-10	21-4	21-10	22-3	22-8	23-1	23-7	24-0	24-5
	24.0	16-5	16-11	17-4	17-10	18-3	18-8	19-1	19-6	19-11	20-4	20-8	21-1	21-5	21-10
E	12.0	1.28	1.39	1.51	1.63	1.76	1.88	2.01	2.15	2.28	2.42	2.56			
	16.0	1.11	1.21	1.31	1.41	1.52	1.63	1.74	1.86	1.98	2.10	2.22	2.34	2.47	2.60
	19.2	1.01	1.10	1.20	1.29	1.39	1.49	1.59	1.70	1.80	1.91	2.03	2.14	2.25	2.37
	24.0	0.90	0.99	1.07	1.15	1.24	1.33	1.42	1.52	1.61	1.71	1.81	1.91	2.02	2.12

NOTE: The required modulus of elasticity, *E*, in 1,000,000 pounds per square inch (psi) (× 0.00689 for N/mm^2) is shown at the bottom of this table, is limited to 2.6 million psi (17 914 N/mm^2) and less, and is applicable to all lumber sizes shown. Spans are shown in feet-inches (1 foot = 304.8 mm, 1 inch = 25.4 mm) and are limited to 26 feet (7925 mm) and less.

TABLE 23-IV-R-11—RAFTERS WITH *L*/180 DEFLECTION LIMITATION

The allowable bending stress (F_b) and modulus of elasticity (*E*) used in this table shall be from Tables 23-IV-V-1 and 23-IV-V-2 only.

DESIGN CRITERIA:
Strength — Live load of 20 psf (0.96 kN/m^2) plus dead load of 20 psf (0.96 kN/m^2) determines the required bending design value.
Deflection — For 20 psf (0.96 kN/m^2) live load.
Limited to span in inches (mm) divided by 180.

Rafter Size (in)	Spacing (in)	Bending Design Value, F_b (psi) × 0.00689 for N/mm²														
× 25.4 for mm		200	300	400	500	600	700	800	900	1000	1100	1200	1300	1400	1500	1600
2 × 4	12.0	3-2	3-11	4-6	5-1	5-6	6-0	6-5	6-9	7-2	7-6	7-10	8-2	8-5	8-9	9-0
	16.0	2-9	3-5	3-11	4-4	4-10	5-2	5-6	5-10	6-2	6-6	6-9	7-1	7-4	7-7	7-10
	19.2	2-6	3-1	3-7	4-0	4-4	4-9	5-1	5-4	5-8	5-11	6-2	6-5	6-8	6-11	7-2
	24.0	2-3	2-9	3-2	3-7	3-11	4-3	4-6	4-10	5-1	5-4	5-6	5-9	6-0	6-2	6-5
2 × 6	12.0	5-0	6-2	7-1	7-11	8-8	9-5	10-0	10-8	11-3	11-9	12-4	12-10	13-3	13-9	14-2
	16.0	4-4	5-4	6-2	6-10	7-6	8-2	8-8	9-3	9-9	10-2	10-8	11-1	11-6	11-11	12-4
	19.2	4-0	4-10	5-7	6-3	6-10	7-5	7-11	8-5	8-11	9-4	9-9	10-1	10-6	10-10	11-3
	24.0	3-7	4-4	5-0	5-7	6-2	6-8	7-1	7-6	7-11	8-4	8-8	9-1	9-5	9-9	10-0
2 × 8	12.0	6-7	8-1	9-4	10-6	11-6	12-5	13-3	14-0	14-10	15-6	16-3	16-10	17-6	18-1	18-9
	16.0	5-9	7-0	8-1	9-1	9-11	10-9	11-6	12-2	12-10	13-5	14-0	14-7	15-2	15-8	16-3
	19.2	5-3	6-5	7-5	8-3	9-1	9-9	10-6	11-1	11-8	12-3	12-10	13-4	13-10	14-4	14-10
	24.0	4-8	5-9	6-7	7-5	8-1	8-9	9-4	9-11	10-6	11-0	11-6	11-11	12-5	12-10	13-3
2 × 10	12.0	8-5	10-4	11-11	13-4	14-8	15-10	16-11	17-11	18-11	19-10	20-8	21-6	22-4	23-1	23-11
	16.0	7-4	8-11	10-4	11-7	12-8	13-8	14-8	15-6	16-4	17-2	17-11	18-8	19-4	20-0	20-8
	19.2	6-8	8-2	9-5	10-7	11-7	12-6	13-4	14-2	14-11	15-8	16-4	17-0	17-8	18-3	18-11
	24.0	6-0	7-4	8-5	9-5	10-4	11-2	11-11	12-8	13-4	14-0	14-8	15-3	15-10	16-4	16-11
E	12.0	0.04	0.08	0.12	0.16	0.21	0.27	0.33	0.39	0.46	0.53	0.60	0.68	0.76	0.84	0.93
	16.0	0.04	0.07	0.10	0.14	0.18	0.23	0.28	0.34	0.40	0.46	0.52	0.59	0.66	0.73	0.80
	19.2	0.03	0.06	0.09	0.13	0.17	0.21	0.26	0.31	0.36	0.42	0.48	0.54	0.60	0.67	0.73
	24.0	0.03	0.05	0.08	0.11	0.15	0.19	0.23	0.28	0.32	0.37	0.43	0.48	0.54	0.60	0.66

Rafter Size (in)	Spacing (in)	Bending Design Value, F_b (psi) × 0.00689 for N/mm²													
× 25.4 for mm		1700	1800	1900	2000	2100	2200	2300	2400	2500	2600	2700	2800	2900	3000
2 × 4	12.0	9-4	9-7	9-10	10-1	10-4	10-7	10-10	11-1	11-4	11-6	11-9	11-11	12-2	12-4
	16.0	8-1	8-4	8-6	8-9	9-0	9-2	9-5	9-7	9-9	10-0	10-2	10-4	10-6	10-9
	19.2	7-4	7-7	7-9	8-0	8-2	8-5	8-7	8-9	8-11	9-1	9-3	9-5	9-7	9-9
	24.0	6-7	6-9	7-0	7-2	7-4	7-6	7-8	7-10	8-0	8-2	8-4	8-5	8-7	8-9
2 × 6	12.0	14-8	15-1	15-6	15-11	16-3	16-8	17-0	17-5	17-9	18-1	18-5	18-9	19-1	19-5
	16.0	12-8	13-1	13-5	13-9	14-1	14-5	14-9	15-1	15-4	15-8	16-0	16-3	16-7	16-10
	19.2	11-7	11-11	12-3	12-7	12-10	13-2	13-6	13-9	14-0	14-4	14-7	14-10	15-1	15-4
	24.0	10-4	10-8	10-11	11-3	11-6	11-9	12-0	12-4	12-7	12-10	13-1	13-3	13-6	13-9
2 × 8	12.0	19-4	19-10	20-5	20-11	21-5	21-11	22-5	22-11	23-5	23-10	24-4	24-9	25-2	25-8
	16.0	16-9	17-2	17-8	18-1	18-7	19-0	19-5	19-10	20-3	20-8	21-1	21-5	21-10	22-2
	19.2	15-3	15-8	16-2	16-7	16-11	17-4	17-9	18-1	18-6	18-10	19-3	19-7	19-11	20-3
	24.0	13-8	14-0	14-5	14-10	15-2	15-6	15-10	16-3	16-7	16-10	17-2	17-6	17-10	18-1
2 × 10	12.0	24-7	25-4	26-0											
	16.0	21-4	21-11	22-6	23-1	23-8	24-3	24-10	25-4	25-10					
	19.2	19-6	20-0	20-7	21-1	21-8	22-2	22-8	23-1	23-7	24-1	24-6	25-0	25-5	25-10
	24.0	17-5	17-11	18-5	18-11	19-4	19-10	20-3	20-8	21-1	21-6	21-11	22-4	22-9	23-1
E	12.0	1.02	1.11	1.20	1.30	1.40	1.50	1.60	1.71	1.82	1.93	2.04	2.15	2.27	2.39
	16.0	0.88	0.96	1.04	1.13	1.21	1.30	1.39	1.48	1.57	1.67	1.76	1.86	1.96	2.07
	19.2	0.80	0.88	0.95	1.03	1.10	1.18	1.27	1.35	1.44	1.52	1.61	1.70	1.79	1.89
	24.0	0.72	0.78	0.85	0.92	0.99	1.06	1.13	1.21	1.28	1.36	1.44	1.52	1.60	1.69

NOTE: The required modulus of elasticity, *E*, in 1,000,000 pounds per square inch (psi) (× 0.00689 for N/mm^2) is shown at the bottom of this table, is limited to 2.6 million psi (17 914 N/mm^2) and less, and is applicable to all lumber sizes shown. Spans are shown in feet-inches (1 foot = 304.8 mm, 1 inch = 25.4 mm) and are limited to 26 feet (7925 mm) and less.

TABLE 23-IV-R-12—RAFTERS WITH *L*/180 DEFLECTION LIMITATION

The allowable bending stress (F_b) and modulus of elasticity *(E)* used in this table shall be from Tables 23-IV-V-1 and 23-IV-V-2 only.

DESIGN CRITERIA:
Strength — Live load of 30 psf (1.44 kN/m^2) plus dead load of 20 psf (0.96 kN/m^2) determines the required bending design value.
Deflection — For 30 psf (1.44 kN/m^2) live load.
Limited to span in inches (mm) divided by 180.

Rafter Size (in)	Spacing (in)	Bending Design Value, F_b (psi) × 0.00689 for N/mm^2														
× 25.4 for mm		200	300	400	500	600	700	800	900	1000	1100	1200	1300	1400	1500	1600
2 × 4	12.0	2-10	3-6	4-0	4-6	4-11	5-4	5-9	6-1	6-5	6-8	7-0	7-3	7-7	7-10	8-1
	16.0	2-6	3-0	3-6	3-11	4-3	4-8	4-11	5-3	5-6	5-10	6-1	6-4	6-7	6-9	7-0
	19.2	2-3	2-9	3-2	3-7	3-11	4-3	4-6	4-10	5-1	5-4	5-6	5-9	6-0	6-2	6-5
	24.0	2-0	2-6	2-10	3-2	3-6	3-9	4-0	4-3	4-6	4-9	4-11	5-2	5-4	5-6	5-9
2 × 6	12.0	4-6	5-6	6-4	7-1	7-9	8-5	9-0	9-6	10-0	10-6	11-0	11-5	11-11	12-4	12-8
	16.0	3-11	4-9	5-6	6-2	6-9	7-3	7-9	8-3	8-8	9-1	9-6	9-11	10-3	10-8	11-0
	19.2	3-7	4-4	5-0	5-7	6-2	6-8	7-1	7-6	7-11	8-4	8-8	9-1	9-5	9-9	10-0
	24.0	3-2	3-11	4-6	5-0	5-6	5-11	6-4	6-9	7-1	7-5	7-9	8-1	8-5	8-8	9-0
2 × 8	12.0	5-11	7-3	8-4	9-4	10-3	11-1	11-10	12-7	13-3	13-11	14-6	15-1	15-8	16-3	16-9
	16.0	5-2	6-3	7-3	8-1	8-11	9-7	10-3	10-10	11-6	12-0	12-7	13-1	13-7	14-0	14-6
	19.2	4-8	5-9	6-7	7-5	8-1	8-9	9-4	9-11	10-6	11-0	11-6	11-11	12-5	12-10	13-3
	24.0	4-2	5-2	5-11	6-7	7-3	7-10	8-4	8-11	9-4	9-10	10-3	10-8	11-1	11-6	11-10
2 × 10	12.0	7-7	9-3	10-8	11-11	13-1	14-2	15-1	16-0	16-11	17-9	18-6	19-3	20-0	20-8	21-4
	16.0	6-6	8-0	9-3	10-4	11-4	12-3	13-1	13-10	14-8	15-4	16-0	16-8	17-4	17-11	18-6
	19.2	6-0	7-4	8-5	9-5	10-4	11-2	11-11	12-8	13-4	14-0	14-8	15-3	15-10	16-4	16-11
	24.0	5-4	6-6	7-7	8-5	9-3	10-0	10-8	11-4	11-11	12-6	13-1	13-7	14-2	14-8	15-1
E	12.0	0.04	0.08	0.12	0.17	0.23	0.29	0.35	0.42	0.49	0.57	0.65	0.73	0.82	0.91	1.00
	16.0	0.04	0.07	0.11	0.15	0.20	0.25	0.31	0.36	0.43	0.49	0.56	0.63	0.71	0.78	0.86
	19.2	0.03	0.06	0.10	0.14	0.18	0.23	0.28	0.33	0.39	0.45	0.51	0.58	0.65	0.72	0.79
	24.0	0.03	0.06	0.09	0.12	0.16	0.20	0.25	0.30	0.35	0.40	0.46	0.52	0.58	0.64	0.71

Rafter Size (in)	Spacing (in)	Bending Design Value, F_b (psi) × 0.00689 for N/mm^2													
× 25.4 for mm		1700	1800	1900	2000	2100	2200	2300	2400	2500	2600	2700	2800	2900	3000
2 × 4	12.0	8-4	8-7	8-10	9-0	9-3	9-6	9-8	9-11	10-1	10-4	10-6	10-8	10-11	11-1
	16.0	7-3	7-5	7-8	7-10	8-0	8-2	8-5	8-7	8-9	8-11	9-1	9-3	9-5	9-7
	19.2	6-7	6-9	7-0	7-2	7-4	7-6	7-8	7-10	8-0	8-2	8-4	8-5	8-7	8-9
	24.0	5-11	6-1	6-3	6-5	6-7	6-8	6-10	7-0	7-2	7-3	7-5	7-7	7-8	7-10
2 × 6	12.0	13-1	13-6	13-10	14-2	14-7	14-11	15-3	15-7	15-11	16-2	16-6	16-10	17-1	17-5
	16.0	11-4	11-8	12-0	12-4	12-7	12-11	13-2	13-6	13-9	14-0	14-3	14-7	14-10	15-1
	19.2	10-4	10-8	10-11	11-3	11-6	11-9	12-0	12-4	12-7	12-10	13-1	13-3	13-6	13-9
	24.0	9-3	9-6	9-9	10-0	10-3	10-6	10-9	11-0	11-3	11-5	11-8	11-11	12-1	12-4
2 × 8	12.0	17-3	17-9	18-3	18-9	19-2	19-8	20-1	20-6	20-11	21-4	21-9	22-2	22-6	22-11
	16.0	14-11	15-5	15-10	16-3	16-7	17-0	17-5	17-9	18-1	18-6	18-10	19-2	19-6	19-10
	19.2	13-8	14-0	14-5	14-10	15-2	15-6	15-10	16-3	16-7	16-10	17-2	17-6	17-10	18-1
	24.0	12-2	12-7	12-11	13-3	13-7	13-11	14-2	14-6	14-10	15-1	15-5	15-8	15-11	16-3
2 × 10	12.0	22-0	22-8	23-3	23-11	24-6	25-1	25-7							
	16.0	19-1	19-7	20-2	20-8	21-2	21-8	22-2	22-8	23-1	23-7	24-0	24-6	24-11	25-4
	19.2	17-5	17-11	18-5	18-11	19-4	19-10	20-3	20-8	21-1	21-6	21-11	22-4	22-9	23-1
	24.0	15-7	16-0	16-6	16-11	17-4	17-9	18-1	18-6	18-11	19-3	19-7	20-0	20-4	20-8
E	12.0	1.09	1.19	1.29	1.39	1.50	1.61	1.72	1.83	1.95	2.07	2.19	2.31	2.43	2.56
	16.0	0.95	1.03	1.12	1.21	1.30	1.39	1.49	1.59	1.69	1.79	1.89	2.00	2.11	2.22
	19.2	0.86	0.94	1.02	1.10	1.19	1.27	1.36	1.45	1.54	1.63	1.73	1.83	1.92	2.03
	24.0	0.77	0.84	0.91	0.99	1.06	1.14	1.22	1.30	1.38	1.46	1.55	1.63	1.72	1.81

NOTE: The required modulus of elasticity, *E*, in 1,000,000 pounds per square inch (psi) (× 0.00689 for N/mm^2) is shown at the bottom of this table, is limited to 2.6 million psi (17 914 N/mm^2) and less, and is applicable to all lumber sizes shown. Spans are shown in feet-inches (1 foot = 304.8 mm, 1 inch = 25.4 mm) and are limited to 26 feet (7925 mm) and less.

TABLE 23-IV-V-1—VALUES FOR JOISTS AND RAFTERS—VISUALLY GRADED LUMBER
For use in Tables 23-IV-J-1 through 23-IV-R-12 and UBC Chapter 23, Division VII only.

These "F_b" values are for use where repetitive members are spaced not more than 24 inches (610 mm). For wider spacing, the "F_b" values shall be reduced 13 percent.

Values for surfaced dry or surfaced green lumber apply at 19 percent maximum moisture content in use.

SPECIES AND GRADE	SIZE (inches)	DESIGN VALUE IN BENDING "F_b" psi			MODULUS OF ELASTICITY "E" psi	GRADING RULES AGENCY
		Normal Duration	Snow Loading	7-day Loading		
	× 25.4 for mm	× 0.00689 for N/mm²				
ASPEN						
Select Structural	2 × 4	1,510	1,735	1,885	1,100,000	NELMA NSLB WWPA
No. 1		1,080	1,240	1,350	1,100,000	
No. 2		1,035	1,190	1,295	1,000,000	
No. 3		605	695	755	900,000	
Stud		600	690	750	900,000	
Construction		805	925	1,005	900,000	
Standard		430	495	540	900,000	
Utility		200	230	250	800,000	
Select Structural	2 × 6	1,310	1,505	1,635	1,100,000	
No. 1		935	1,075	1,170	1,100,000	
No. 2		895	1,030	1,120	1,000,000	
No. 3		525	600	655	900,000	
Stud		545	630	685	900,000	
Select Structural	2 × 8	1,210	1,390	1,510	1,100,000	
No. 1		865	990	1,080	1,100,000	
No. 2		830	950	1,035	1,000,000	
No. 3		485	555	605	900,000	
Select Structural	2 × 10	1,105	1,275	1,385	1,100,000	
No. 1		790	910	990	1,100,000	
No. 2		760	875	950	1,000,000	
No. 3		445	510	555	900,000	
Select Structural	2 × 12	1,005	1,155	1,260	1,100,000	
No. 1		720	825	900	1,100,000	
No. 2		690	795	865	1,000,000	
No. 3		405	465	505	900,000	
BEECH-BIRCH-HICKORY						
Select Structural	2 × 4	2,500	2,875	3,125	1,700,000	NELMA
No. 1		1,810	2,085	2,265	1,600,000	
No. 2		1,725	1,985	2,155	1,500,000	
No. 3		990	1,140	1,240	1,300,000	
Stud		980	1,125	1,225	1,300,000	
Construction		1,325	1,520	1,655	1,400,000	
Standard		750	860	935	1,300,000	
Utility		345	395	430	1,200,000	
Select Structural	2 × 6	2,170	2,495	2,710	1,700,000	
No. 1		1,570	1,805	1,960	1,600,000	
No. 2		1,495	1,720	1,870	1,500,000	
No. 3		860	990	1,075	1,300,000	
Stud		890	1,025	1,115	1,300,000	
Select Structural	2 × 8	2,000	2,300	2,500	1,700,000	
No. 1		1,450	1,665	1,810	1,600,000	
No. 2		1,380	1,585	1,725	1,500,000	
No. 3		795	915	990	1,300,000	
Select Structural	2 × 10	1,835	2,110	2,295	1,700,000	
No. 1		1,330	1,525	1,660	1,600,000	
No. 2		1,265	1,455	1,580	1,500,000	
No. 3		725	835	910	1,300,000	
Select Structural	2 × 12	1,670	1,920	2,085	1,700,000	
No. 1		1,210	1,390	1,510	1,600,000	
No. 2		1,150	1,325	1,440	1,500,000	
No. 3		660	760	825	1,300,000	

(Continued)

TABLE 23-IV-V-1—VALUES FOR JOISTS AND RAFTERS—VISUALLY GRADED LUMBER—(Continued)

SPECIES AND GRADE	SIZE (inches)	DESIGN VALUE IN BENDING "F_b" psi			MODULUS OF ELASTICITY "E" psi	GRADING RULES AGENCY
		Normal Duration	Snow Loading	7-day Loading		
	× 25.4 for mm	× 0.00689 for N/mm²				
COTTONWOOD						
Select Structural	2 × 4	1,510	1,735	1,885	1,200,000	NSLB
No. 1		1,080	1,240	1,350	1,200,000	
No. 2		1,080	1,240	1,350	1,100,000	
No. 3		605	695	755	1,000,000	
Stud		600	690	750	1,000,000	
Construction		805	925	1,005	1,000,000	
Standard		460	530	575	900,000	
Utility		200	230	250	900,000	
Select Structural	2 × 6	1,310	1,505	1,635	1,200,000	
No. 1		935	1,075	1,170	1,200,000	
No. 2		935	1,075	1,170	1,100,000	
No. 3		525	600	655	1,000,000	
Stud		545	630	685	1,000,000	
Select Structural	2 × 8	1,210	1,390	1,510	1,200,000	
No. 1		865	990	1,080	1,200,000	
No. 2		865	990	1,080	1,100,000	
No. 3		485	555	605	1,000,000	
Select Structural	2 × 10	1,105	1,275	1,385	1,200,000	
No. 1		790	910	990	1,200,000	
No. 2		790	910	990	1,100,000	
No. 3		445	510	555	1,000,000	
Select Structural	2 × 12	1,005	1,155	1,260	1,200,000	
No. 1		720	825	900	1,200,000	
No. 2		720	825	900	1,100,000	
No. 3		405	465	505	1,000,000	
DOUGLAS FIR-LARCH						
Select Structural	2 × 4	2,500	2,875	3,125	1,900,000	WCLIB WWPA
No. 1 and better		1,985	2,280	2,480	1,800,000	
No. 1		1,725	1,985	2,155	1,700,000	
No. 2		1,510	1,735	1,885	1,600,000	
No. 3		865	990	1,080	1,400,000	
Stud		855	980	1,065	1,400,000	
Construction		1,150	1,325	1,440	1,500,000	
Standard		635	725	790	1,400,000	
Utility		315	365	395	1,300,000	
Select Structural	2 × 6	2,170	2,495	2,710	1,900,000	
No. 1 and better		1,720	1,975	2,150	1,800,000	
No. 1		1,495	1,720	1,870	1,700,000	
No. 2		1,310	1,505	1,635	1,600,000	
No. 3		750	860	935	1,400,000	
Stud		775	895	970	1,400,000	
Select Structural	2 × 8	2,000	2,300	2,500	1,900,000	
No. 1 and better		1,585	1,825	1,985	1,800,000	
No. 1		1,380	1,585	1,725	1,700,000	
No. 2		1,210	1,390	1,510	1,600,000	
No. 3		690	795	865	1,400,000	
Select Structural	2 × 10	1,835	2,110	2,295	1,900,000	
No. 1 and better		1,455	1,675	1,820	1,800,000	
No. 1		1,265	1,455	1,580	1,700,000	
No. 2		1,105	1,275	1,385	1,600,000	
No. 3		635	725	790	1,400,000	
Select Structural	2 × 12	1,670	1,920	2,085	1,900,000	
No. 1 and better		1,325	1,520	1,655	1,800,000	
No. 1		1,150	1,325	1,440	1,700,000	
No. 2		1,005	1,155	1,260	1,600,000	
No. 3		575	660	720	1,400,000	

(Continued)

TABLE 23-IV-V-1—VALUES FOR JOISTS AND RAFTERS—VISUALLY GRADED LUMBER—(Continued)

SPECIES AND GRADE	SIZE (inches)	DESIGN VALUE IN BENDING "F_b" psi: Normal Duration	Snow Loading	7-day Loading	MODULUS OF ELASTICITY "E" psi	GRADING RULES AGENCY
	× 25.4 for mm	× 0.00689 for N/mm²				
DOUGLAS FIR-LARCH (North)						
Select Structural	2 × 4	2,245	2,580	2,805	1,900,000	NLGA
No. 1/No. 2		1,425	1,635	1,780	1,600,000	
No. 3		820	940	1,025	1,400,000	
Stud		820	945	1,030	1,400,000	
Construction		1,095	1,255	1,365	1,500,000	
Standard		605	695	755	1,400,000	
Utility		290	330	360	1,300,000	
Select Structural	2 × 6	1,945	2,235	2,430	1,900,000	
No. 1/No. 2		1,235	1,420	1,540	1,600,000	
No. 3		710	815	890	1,400,000	
Stud		750	860	935	1,400,000	
Select Structural	2 × 8	1,795	2,065	2,245	1,900,000	
No. 1/No. 2		1,140	1,310	1,425	1,600,000	
No. 3		655	755	820	1,400,000	
Select Structural	2 × 10	1,645	1,890	2,055	1,900,000	
No. 1/No. 2		1,045	1,200	1,305	1,600,000	
No. 3		600	690	750	1,400,000	
Select Structural	2 × 12	1,495	1,720	1,870	1,900,000	
No. 1/No. 2		950	1,090	1,185	1,600,000	
No. 3		545	630	685	1,400,000	
DOUGLAS FIR (South)						
Select Structural	2 × 4	2,245	2,580	2,805	1,400,000	WWPA
No. 1		1,555	1,785	1,940	1,300,000	
No. 2		1,425	1,635	1,780	1,200,000	
No. 3		820	940	1,025	1,100,000	
Stud		820	945	1,030	1,100,000	
Construction		1,065	1,225	1,330	1,200,000	
Standard		605	695	755	1,100,000	
Utility		290	330	360	1,000,000	
Select Structural	2 × 6	1,945	2,235	2,430	1,400,000	
No. 1		1,345	1,545	1,680	1,300,000	
No. 2		1,235	1,420	1,540	1,200,000	
No. 3		710	815	890	1,100,000	
Stud		750	860	935	1,100,000	
Select Structural	2 × 8	1,795	2,065	2,245	1,400,000	
No. 1		1,240	1,430	1,555	1,300,000	
No. 2		1,140	1,310	1,425	1,200,000	
No. 3		655	755	820	1,100,000	
Select Structural	2 × 10	1,645	1,890	2,055	1,400,000	
No. 1		1,140	1,310	1,425	1,300,000	
No. 2		1,045	1,200	1,305	1,200,000	
No. 3		600	690	750	1,100,000	
Select Structural	2 × 12	1,495	1,720	1,870	1,400,000	
No. 1		1,035	1,190	1,295	1,300,000	
No. 2		950	1,090	1,185	1,200,000	
No. 3		545	630	685	1,100,000	

(Continued)

TABLE 23-IV-V-1—VALUES FOR JOISTS AND RAFTERS—VISUALLY GRADED LUMBER—(Continued)

SPECIES AND GRADE	SIZE (inches)	DESIGN VALUE IN BENDING "F_b" psi			MODULUS OF ELASTICITY "E" psi	GRADING RULES AGENCY
		Normal Duration	Snow Loading	7-day Loading		
	× 25.4 for mm	× 0.00689 for N/mm²				
EASTERN HEMLOCK—TAMARACK						
Select Structural	2 × 4	2,155	2,480	2,695	1,200,000	NELMA NSLB
No. 1		1,335	1,535	1,670	1,100,000	
No. 2		990	1,140	1,240	1,100,000	
No. 3		605	695	755	900,000	
Stud		570	655	710	900,000	
Construction		775	895	970	1,000,000	
Standard		430	495	540	900,000	
Utility		200	230	250	800,000	
Select Structural	2 × 6	1,870	2,150	2,335	1,200,000	
No. 1		1,160	1,330	1,450	1,100,000	
No. 2		860	990	1,075	1,100,000	
No. 3		525	600	655	900,000	
Stud		520	595	645	900,000	
Select Structural	2 × 8	1,725	1,985	2,155	1,200,000	
No. 1		1,070	1,230	1,335	1,100,000	
No. 2		795	915	990	1,100,000	
No. 3		485	555	605	900,000	
Select Structural	2 × 10	1,580	1,820	1,975	1,200,000	
No. 1		980	1,125	1,225	1,100,000	
No. 2		725	835	910	1,100,000	
No. 3		445	510	555	900,000	
Select Structural	2 × 12	1,440	1,655	1,795	1,200,000	
No. 1		890	1,025	1,115	1,100,000	
No. 2		660	760	825	1,100,000	
No. 3		405	465	505	900,000	
EASTERN SOFTWOODS						
Select Structural	2 × 4	2,155	2,480	2,695	1,200,000	NELMA NSLB
No. 1		1,335	1,535	1,670	1,100,000	
No. 2		990	1,140	1,240	1,100,000	
No. 3		605	695	755	900,000	
Stud		570	655	710	900,000	
Construction		775	895	970	1,000,000	
Standard		430	495	540	900,000	
Utility		200	230	250	800,000	
Select Structural	2 × 6	1,870	2,150	2,335	1,200,000	
No. 1		1,160	1,330	1,450	1,100,000	
No. 2		860	990	1,075	1,100,000	
No. 3		525	600	655	900,000	
Stud		520	595	645	900,000	
Select Structural	2 × 8	1,725	1,985	2,155	1,200,000	
No. 1		1,070	1,230	1,335	1,100,000	
No. 2		795	915	990	1,100,000	
No. 3		485	555	605	900,000	
Select Structural	2 × 10	1,580	1,820	1,975	1,200,000	
No. 1		980	1,125	1,225	1,100,000	
No. 2		725	835	910	1,100,000	
No. 3		445	510	555	900,000	
Select Structural	2 × 12	1,440	1,655	1,795	1,200,000	
No. 1		890	1,025	1,115	1,100,000	
No. 2		660	760	825	1,100,000	
No. 3		405	465	505	900,000	

(Continued)

TABLE 23-IV-V-1—VALUES FOR JOISTS AND RAFTERS—VISUALLY GRADED LUMBER—(Continued)

SPECIES AND GRADE	SIZE (inches)	DESIGN VALUE IN BENDING "F_b" psi			MODULUS OF ELASTICITY "E" psi	GRADING RULES AGENCY
		Normal Duration	Snow Loading	7-day Loading		
	× 25.4 for mm	× 0.00689 for N/mm²				
EASTERN WHITE PINE						
Select Structural	2 × 4	2,155	2,480	2,695	1,200,000	NELMA NSLB
No. 1		1,335	1,535	1,670	1,100,000	
No. 2		990	1,140	1,240	1,100,000	
No. 3		605	695	755	900,000	
Stud		570	655	710	900,000	
Construction		775	895	970	1,000,000	
Standard		430	495	540	900,000	
Utility		200	230	250	800,000	
Select Structural	2 × 6	1,870	2,150	2,335	1,200,000	
No. 1		1,160	1,330	1,450	1,100,000	
No. 2		860	990	1,075	1,100,000	
No. 3		525	600	655	900,000	
Stud		520	595	645	900,000	
Select Structural	2 × 8	1,725	1,985	2,155	1,200,000	
No. 1		1,070	1,230	1,335	1,100,000	
No. 2		795	915	990	1,100,000	
No. 3		485	555	605	900,000	
Select Structural	2 × 10	1,580	1,820	1,975	1,200,000	
No. 1		980	1,125	1,225	1,100,000	
No. 2		725	835	910	1,100,000	
No. 3		445	510	555	900,000	
Select Structural	2 × 12	1,440	1,655	1,795	1,200,000	
No. 1		890	1,025	1,115	1,100,000	
No. 2		660	760	825	1,100,000	
No. 3		405	465	505	900,000	
HEM-FIR						
Select Structural	2 × 4	2,415	2,775	3,020	1,600,000	WCLIB WWPA
No. 1 and better		1,810	2,085	2,265	1,500,000	
No. 1		1,640	1,885	2,050	1,500,000	
No. 2		1,465	1,685	1,835	1,300,000	
No. 3		865	990	1,080	1,200,000	
Stud		855	980	1,065	1,200,000	
Construction		1,120	1,290	1,400	1,300,000	
Standard		635	725	790	1,200,000	
Utility		290	330	360	1,100,000	
Select Structural	2 × 6	2,095	2,405	2,615	1,600,000	
No. 1 and better		1,570	1,805	1,960	1,500,000	
No. 1		1,420	1,635	1,775	1,500,000	
No. 2		1,270	1,460	1,590	1,300,000	
No. 3		750	860	935	1,200,000	
Stud		775	895	970	1,200,000	
Select Structural	2 × 8	1,930	2,220	2,415	1,600,000	
No. 1 and better		1,450	1,665	1,810	1,500,000	
No. 1		1,310	1,510	1,640	1,500,000	
No. 2		1,175	1,350	1,465	1,300,000	
No. 3		690	795	865	1,200,000	
Select Structural	2 × 10	1,770	2,035	2,215	1,600,000	
No. 1 and better		1,330	1,525	1,660	1,500,000	
No. 1		1,200	1,380	1,500	1,500,000	
No. 2		1,075	1,235	1,345	1,300,000	
No. 3		635	725	790	1,200,000	
Select Structural	2 × 12	1,610	1,850	2,015	1,600,000	
No. 1 and better		1,210	1,390	1,510	1,500,000	
No. 1		1,095	1,255	1,365	1,500,000	
No. 2		980	1,125	1,220	1,300,000	
No. 3		575	660	720	1,200,000	

(Continued)

TABLE 23-IV-V-1—VALUES FOR JOISTS AND RAFTERS—VISUALLY GRADED LUMBER—(Continued)

SPECIES AND GRADE	SIZE (inches) × 25.4 for mm	DESIGN VALUE IN BENDING "F_b" psi Normal Duration	Snow Loading	7-day Loading	MODULUS OF ELASTICITY "E" psi	GRADING RULES AGENCY
		× 0.00689 for N/mm²				
HEM-FIR (North)						
Select Structural	2 × 4	2,245	2,580	2,805	1,700,000	NLGA
No. 1/No. 2		1,725	1,985	2,155	1,600,000	
No. 3		990	1,140	1,240	1,400,000	
Stud		980	1,125	1,225	1,400,000	
Construction		1,325	1,520	1,655	1,500,000	
Standard		720	825	900	1,400,000	
Utility		345	395	430	1,300,000	
Select Structural	2 × 6	1,945	2,235	2,430	1,700,000	
No. 1/No. 2		1,495	1,720	1,870	1,600,000	
No. 3		860	990	1,075	1,400,000	
Stud		890	1,025	1,115	1,400,000	
Select Structural	2 × 8	1,795	2,065	2,245	1,700,000	
No. 1/No. 2		1,380	1,585	1,725	1,600,000	
No. 3		795	915	990	1,400,000	
Select Structural	2 × 10	1,645	1,890	2,055	1,700,000	
No. 1/No. 2		1,265	1,455	1,580	1,600,000	
No. 3		725	835	910	1,400,000	
Select Structural	2 × 12	1,495	1,720	1,870	1,700,000	
No. 1/No. 2		1,150	1,325	1,440	1,600,000	
No. 3		660	760	825	1,400,000	
MIXED MAPLE						
Select Structural	2 × 4	1,725	1,985	2,155	1,300,000	NELMA
No. 1		1,250	1,440	1,565	1,200,000	
No. 2		1,210	1,390	1,510	1,100,000	
No. 3		690	795	865	1,000,000	
Stud		695	800	870	1,000,000	
Construction		920	1,060	1,150	1,100,000	
Standard		520	595	645	1,000,000	
Utility		260	300	325	900,000	
Select Structural	2 × 6	1,495	1,720	1,870	1,300,000	
No. 1		1,085	1,245	1,355	1,200,000	
No. 2		1,045	1,205	1,310	1,100,000	
No. 3		600	690	750	1,000,000	
Stud		635	725	790	1,000,000	
Select Structural	2 × 8	1,380	1,585	1,725	1,300,000	
No. 1		1,000	1,150	1,250	1,200,000	
No. 2		965	1,110	1,210	1,100,000	
No. 3		550	635	690	1,000,000	
Select Structural	2 × 10	1,265	1,455	1,580	1,300,000	
No. 1		915	1,055	1,145	1,200,000	
No. 2		885	1,020	1,105	1,100,000	
No. 3		505	580	635	1,000,000	
Select Structural	2 × 12	1,150	1,325	1,440	1,300,000	
No. 1		835	960	1,040	1,200,000	
No. 2		805	925	1,005	1,100,000	
No. 3		460	530	575	1,000,000	
MIXED OAK						
Select Structural	2 × 4	1,985	2,280	2,480	1,100,000	NELMA
No. 1		1,425	1,635	1,780	1,000,000	
No. 2		1,380	1,585	1,725	900,000	
No. 3		820	940	1,025	800,000	
Stud		790	910	990	800,000	
Construction		1,065	1,225	1,330	900,000	
Standard		605	695	755	800,000	
Utility		290	330	360	800,000	

(Continued)

TABLE 23-IV-V-1—VALUES FOR JOISTS AND RAFTERS—VISUALLY GRADED LUMBER—(Continued)

SPECIES AND GRADE	SIZE (inches)	DESIGN VALUE IN BENDING "F_b" psi			MODULUS OF ELASTICITY "E" psi	GRADING RULES AGENCY
		Normal Duration	Snow Loading	7-day Loading		
	× 25.4 for mm	× 0.00689 for N/mm²				
MIXED OAK—(continued)						
Select Structural	2 × 6	1,720	1,975	2,150	1,100,000	NELMA
No. 1	2 × 6	1,235	1,420	1,540	1,000,000	NELMA
No. 2	2 × 6	1,195	1,375	1,495	900,000	NELMA
No. 3	2 × 6	710	815	890	800,000	NELMA
Stud	2 × 6	720	825	900	800,000	NELMA
Select Structural	2 × 8	1,585	1,825	1,985	1,100,000	NELMA
No. 1	2 × 8	1,140	1,310	1,425	1,000,000	NELMA
No. 2	2 × 8	1,105	1,270	1,380	900,000	NELMA
No. 3	2 × 8	655	755	820	800,000	NELMA
Select Structural	2 × 10	1,455	1,675	1,820	1,100,000	NELMA
No. 1	2 × 10	1,045	1,200	1,305	1,000,000	NELMA
No. 2	2 × 10	1,010	1,165	1,265	900,000	NELMA
No. 3	2 × 10	600	690	750	800,000	NELMA
Select Structural	2 × 12	1,325	1,520	1,655	1,100,000	NELMA
No. 1	2 × 12	950	1,090	1,185	1,000,000	NELMA
No. 2	2 × 12	920	1,060	1,150	900,000	NELMA
No. 3	2 × 12	545	630	685	800,000	NELMA
MIXED SOUTHERN PINE						
Select Structural	2 × 4	2,360	2,710	2,950	1,600,000	SPIB
No. 1	2 × 4	1,670	1,920	2,080	1,500,000	SPIB
No. 2	2 × 4	1,500	1,720	1,870	1,400,000	SPIB
No. 3	2 × 4	865	990	1,080	1,200,000	SPIB
Stud	2 × 4	890	1,020	1,110	1,200,000	SPIB
Construction	2 × 4	1,150	1,320	1,440	1,300,000	SPIB
Standard	2 × 4	635	725	790	1,200,000	SPIB
Utility	2 × 4	315	365	395	1,100,000	SPIB
Select Structural	2 × 6	2,130	2,450	2,660	1,600,000	SPIB
No. 1	2 × 6	1,490	1,720	1,870	1,500,000	SPIB
No. 2	2 × 6	1,320	1,520	1,650	1,400,000	SPIB
No. 3	2 × 6	775	895	970	1,200,000	SPIB
Stud	2 × 6	775	895	970	1,200,000	SPIB
Select Structural	2 × 8	2,010	2,310	2,520	1,600,000	SPIB
No. 1	2 × 8	1,380	1,590	1,720	1,500,000	SPIB
No. 2	2 × 8	1,210	1,390	1,510	1,400,000	SPIB
No. 3	2 × 8	720	825	900	1,200,000	SPIB
Select Structural	2 × 10	1,730	1,980	2,160	1,600,000	SPIB
No. 1	2 × 10	1,210	1,390	1,510	1,500,000	SPIB
No. 2	2 × 10	1,060	1,220	1,330	1,400,000	SPIB
No. 3	2 × 10	605	695	755	1,200,000	SPIB
Select Structural	2 × 12	1,610	1,850	2,010	1,600,000	SPIB
No. 1	2 × 12	1,120	1,290	1,400	1,500,000	SPIB
No. 2	2 × 12	1,010	1,160	1,260	1,400,000	SPIB
No. 3	2 × 12	575	660	720	1,200,000	SPIB

(Continued)

TABLE 23-IV-V-1—VALUES FOR JOISTS AND RAFTERS—VISUALLY GRADED LUMBER—(Continued)

SPECIES AND GRADE	SIZE (inches) × 25.4 for mm	DESIGN VALUE IN BENDING "F_b" psi — Normal Duration	Snow Loading	7-day Loading	MODULUS OF ELASTICITY "E" psi	GRADING RULES AGENCY
		× 0.00689 for N/mm²				
NORTHERN RED OAK						
Select Structural	2 × 4	2,415	2,775	3,020	1,400,000	NELMA
No. 1	2 × 4	1,725	1,985	2,155	1,400,000	NELMA
No. 2	2 × 4	1,680	1,935	2,100	1,300,000	NELMA
No. 3	2 × 4	950	1,090	1,185	1,200,000	NELMA
Stud	2 × 4	950	1,090	1,185	1,200,000	NELMA
Construction	2 × 4	1,265	1,455	1,580	1,200,000	NELMA
Standard	2 × 4	720	825	900	1,100,000	NELMA
Utility	2 × 4	345	395	430	1,000,000	NELMA
Select Structural	2 × 6	2,095	2,405	2,615	1,400,000	NELMA
No. 1	2 × 6	1,495	1,720	1,870	1,400,000	NELMA
No. 2	2 × 6	1,460	1,675	1,820	1,300,000	NELMA
No. 3	2 × 6	820	945	1,030	1,200,000	NELMA
Stud	2 × 6	865	990	1,080	1,200,000	NELMA
Select Structural	2 × 8	1,930	2,220	2,415	1,400,000	NELMA
No. 1	2 × 8	1,380	1,585	1,725	1,400,000	NELMA
No. 2	2 × 8	1,345	1,545	1,680	1,300,000	NELMA
No. 3	2 × 8	760	875	950	1,200,000	NELMA
Select Structural	2 × 10	1,770	2,035	2,215	1,400,000	NELMA
No. 1	2 × 10	1,265	1,455	1,580	1,400,000	NELMA
No. 2	2 × 10	1,235	1,420	1,540	1,300,000	NELMA
No. 3	2 × 10	695	800	870	1,200,000	NELMA
Select Structural	2 × 12	1,610	1,850	2,015	1,400,000	NELMA
No. 1	2 × 12	1,150	1,325	1,440	1,400,000	NELMA
No. 2	2 × 12	1,120	1,290	1,400	1,300,000	NELMA
No. 3	2 × 12	635	725	790	1,200,000	NELMA
NORTHERN SPECIES						
Select Structural	2 × 4	1,640	1,885	2,050	1,100,000	NLGA
No. 1/No. 2	2 × 4	990	1,140	1,240	1,100,000	NLGA
No. 3	2 × 4	605	695	755	1,000,000	NLGA
Stud	2 × 4	570	655	710	1,000,000	NLGA
Construction	2 × 4	775	895	970	1,000,000	NLGA
Standard	2 × 4	430	495	540	900,000	NLGA
Utility	2 × 4	200	230	250	900,000	NLGA
Select Structural	2 × 6	1,420	1,635	1,775	1,100,000	NLGA
No. 1/No. 2	2 × 6	860	990	1,075	1,100,000	NLGA
No. 3	2 × 6	525	600	655	1,000,000	NLGA
Stud	2 × 6	520	595	645	1,000,000	NLGA
Select Structural	2 × 8	1,310	1,510	1,640	1,100,000	NLGA
No. 1/No. 2	2 × 8	795	915	990	1,100,000	NLGA
No. 3	2 × 8	485	555	605	1,000,000	NLGA
Select Structural	2 × 10	1,200	1,380	1,500	1,100,000	NLGA
No. 1/No. 2	2 × 10	725	835	910	1,100,000	NLGA
No. 3	2 × 10	445	510	555	1,000,000	NLGA
Select Structural	2 × 12	1,095	1,255	1,365	1,100,000	NLGA
No. 1/No. 2	2 × 12	660	760	825	1,100,000	NLGA
No. 3	2 × 12	405	465	505	1,000,000	NLGA

(Continued)

TABLE 23-IV-V-1—VALUES FOR JOISTS AND RAFTERS—VISUALLY GRADED LUMBER—(Continued)

SPECIES AND GRADE	SIZE (inches)	DESIGN VALUE IN BENDING "F_b" psi			MODULUS OF ELASTICITY "E" psi	GRADING RULES AGENCY
		Normal Duration	Snow Loading	7-day Loading		
	× 25.4 for mm	× 0.00689 for N/mm²				
NORTHERN WHITE CEDAR						
Select Structural	2 × 4	1,335	1,535	1,670	800,000	NELMA
No. 1		990	1,140	1,240	700,000	
No. 2		950	1,090	1,185	700,000	
No. 3		560	645	700	600,000	
Stud		540	620	670	600,000	
Construction		720	825	900	700,000	
Standard		405	465	505	600,000	
Utility		200	230	250	600,000	
Select Structural	2 × 6	1,160	1,330	1,450	800,000	
No. 1		860	990	1,075	700,000	
No. 2		820	945	1,030	700,000	
No. 3		485	560	605	600,000	
Stud		490	560	610	600,000	
Select Structural	2 × 8	1,070	1,230	1,335	800,000	
No. 1		795	915	990	700,000	
No. 2		760	875	950	700,000	
No. 3		450	515	560	600,000	
Select Structural	2 × 10	980	1,125	1,225	800,000	
No. 1		725	835	910	700,000	
No. 2		695	800	870	700,000	
No. 3		410	475	515	600,000	
Select Structural	2 × 12	890	1,025	1,115	800,000	
No. 1		660	760	825	700,000	
No. 2		635	725	790	700,000	
No. 3		375	430	465	600,000	
RED MAPLE						
Select Structural	2 × 4	2,245	2,580	2,805	1,700,000	NELMA
No. 1		1,595	1,835	1,995	1,600,000	
No. 2		1,555	1,785	1,940	1,500,000	
No. 3		905	1,040	1,130	1,300,000	
Stud		885	1,020	1,105	1,300,000	
Construction		1,210	1,390	1,510	1,400,000	
Standard		660	760	825	1,300,000	
Utility		315	365	395	1,200,000	
Select Structural	2 × 6	1,945	2,235	2,430	1,700,000	
No. 1		1,385	1,590	1,730	1,600,000	
No. 2		1,345	1,545	1,680	1,500,000	
No. 3		785	905	980	1,300,000	
Stud		805	925	1,005	1,300,000	
Select Structural	2 × 8	1,795	2,065	2,245	1,700,000	
No. 1		1,275	1,470	1,595	1,600,000	
No. 2		1,240	1,430	1,555	1,500,000	
No. 3		725	835	905	1,300,000	
Select Structural	2 × 10	1,645	1,890	2,055	1,700,000	
No. 1		1,170	1,345	1,465	1,600,000	
No. 2		1,140	1,310	1,425	1,500,000	
No. 3		665	765	830	1,300,000	
Select Structural	2 × 12	1,495	1,720	1,870	1,700,000	
No. 1		1,065	1,225	1,330	1,600,000	
No. 2		1,035	1,190	1,295	1,500,000	
No. 3		605	695	755	1,300,000	

(Continued)

TABLE 23-IV-V-1—VALUES FOR JOISTS AND RAFTERS—VISUALLY GRADED LUMBER—(Continued)

SPECIES AND GRADE	SIZE (inches)	DESIGN VALUE IN BENDING "F_b" psi			MODULUS OF ELASTICITY "E" psi	GRADING RULES AGENCY
		Normal Duration	Snow Loading	7-day Loading		
	× 25.4 for mm	× 0.00689 for N/mm²				
RED OAK						
Select Structural	2 × 4	1,985	2,280	2,480	1,400,000	NELMA
No. 1		1,425	1,635	1,780	1,300,000	
No. 2		1,380	1,585	1,725	1,200,000	
No. 3		820	940	1,025	1,100,000	
Stud		790	910	990	1,100,006	
Construction		1,065	1,225	1,330	1,200,000	
Standard		605	695	755	1,100,000	
Utility		290	330	360	1,000,000	
Select Structural	2 × 6	1,720	1,975	2,150	1,400,000	
No. 1		1,235	1,420	1,540	1,300,000	
No. 2		1,195	1,375	1,495	1,200,000	
No. 3		710	815	890	1,100,000	
Stud		720	825	900	1,100,000	
Select Structural	2 × 8	1,585	1,825	1,985	1,400,000	
No. 1		1,140	1,310	1,425	1,300,000	
No. 2		1,105	1,270	1,380	1,200,000	
No. 3		655	755	820	1,100,000	
Select Structural	2 × 10	1,455	1,675	1,820	1,400,000	
No. 1		1,045	1,200	1,305	1,300,000	
No. 2		1,010	1,165	1,265	1,200,000	
No. 3		600	690	750	1,100,000	
Select Structural	2 × 12	1,325	1,520	1,655	1,400,000	
No. 1		950	1,090	1,185	1,300,000	
No. 2		920	1,060	1,150	1,200,000	
No. 3		545	630	685	1,100,000	
REDWOOD						
Clear Structural	2 × 4	3,020	3,470	3,775	1,400,000	RIS
Select Structural		2,330	2,680	2,910	1,400,000	
Select Structural, open grain		1,900	2,180	2,370	1,100,000	
No. 1		1,680	1,935	2,100	1,300,000	
No. 1, open grain		1,335	1,535	1,670	1,100,000	
No. 2		1,595	1,835	1,995	1,200,000	
No. 2, open grain		1,250	1,440	1,565	1,000,000	
No. 3		905	1,040	1,130	1,100,000	
No. 3, open grain		735	845	915	900,000	
Stud		725	835	910	900,000	
Construction		950	1,090	1,185	900,000	
Standard		520	595	645	900,000	
Utility		260	300	325	800,000	
Clear Structural	2 × 6	2,615	3,010	3,270	1,400,000	
Select Structural		2,020	2,320	2,525	1,400,000	
Select Structural, open grain		1,645	1,890	2,055	1,100,000	
No. 1		1,460	1,675	1,820	1,300,000	
No. 1, open grain		1,160	1,330	1,450	1,100,000	
No. 2		1,385	1,590	1,730	1,200,000	
No. 2, open grain		1,085	1,245	1,355	1,000,000	
No. 3		785	905	980	1,100,000	
No. 3, open grain		635	730	795	900,000	
Stud		660	760	825	900,000	

(Continued)

TABLE 23-IV-V-1—VALUES FOR JOISTS AND RAFTERS—VISUALLY GRADED LUMBER—(Continued)

SPECIES AND GRADE	SIZE (inches)	DESIGN VALUE IN BENDING "F_b" psi			MODULUS OF ELASTICITY "E" psi	GRADING RULES AGENCY
		Normal Duration	Snow Loading	7-day Loading		
	× 25.4 for mm	× 0.00689 for N/mm²				
REDWOOD—(continued)						
Clear Structural	2 × 8	2,415	2,775	3,020	1,400,000	RIS
Select Structural		1,865	2,140	2,330	1,400,000	
Select Structural, open grain		1,520	1,745	1,900	1,100,000	
No. 1		1,345	1,545	1,680	1,300,000	
No. 1, open grain		1,070	1,230	1,335	1,100,000	
No. 2		1,275	1,470	1,595	1,200,000	
No. 2, open grain		1,000	1,150	1,250	1,000,000	
No. 3		725	835	905	1,100,000	
No. 3, open grain		585	675	735	900,000	
Clear Structural	2 × 10	2,215	2,545	2,765	1,400,000	
Select Structural		1,710	1,965	2,135	1,400,000	
Select Structural, open grain		1,390	1,600	1,740	1,100,000	
No. 1		1,235	1,420	1,540	1,300,000	
No. 1, open grain		980	1,125	1,225	1,100,000	
No. 2		1,170	1,345	1,465	1,200,000	
No. 2, open grain		915	1,055	1,145	1,000,000	
No. 3		665	765	830	1,100,000	
No. 3, open grain		540	620	670	900,000	
Clear Structural	2 × 12	2,015	2,315	2,515	1,400,000	
Select Structural		1,555	1,785	1,940	1,400,000	
Select Structural, open grain		1,265	1,455	1,580	1,100,000	
No. 1		1,120	1,290	1,400	1,300,000	
No. 1, open grain		890	1,025	1,115	1,100,000	
No. 2		1,065	1,225	1,330	1,200,000	
No. 2, open grain		835	960	1,040	1,000,000	
No. 3		605	695	755	1,100,000	
No. 3, open grain		490	560	610	900,000	
SOUTHERN PINE						
Dense Select Structural	2 × 4	3,510	4,030	4,380	1,900,000	SPIB
Select Structural		3,280	3,770	4,100	1,800,000	
Non-Dense Select Structural		3,050	3,500	3,810	1,700,000	
No. 1 Dense		2,300	2,650	2,880	1,800,000	
No. 1		2,130	2,450	2,660	1,700,000	
No. 1 Non-Dense		1,950	2,250	2,440	1,600,000	
No. 2 Dense		1,960	2,250	2,440	1,700,000	
No. 2		1,720	1,980	2,160	1,600,000	
No. 2 Non-Dense		1,550	1,790	1,940	1,400,000	
No. 3		980	1,120	1,220	1,400,000	
Stud		1,010	1,160	1,260	1,400,000	
Construction		1,270	1,450	1,580	1,500,000	
Standard		720	825	900	1,300,000	
Utility		345	395	430	1,300,000	

(Continued)

TABLE 23-IV-V-1—VALUES FOR JOISTS AND RAFTERS—VISUALLY GRADED LUMBER—(Continued)

SPECIES AND GRADE	SIZE (inches)	DESIGN VALUE IN BENDING "F_b" psi			MODULUS OF ELASTICITY "E" psi	GRADING RULES AGENCY
		Normal Duration	Snow Loading	7-day Loading		
	× 25.4 for mm	× 0.00689 for N/mm²				
SOUTHERN PINE—(continued)						
Dense Select Structural	2 × 6	3,100	3,570	3,880	1,900,000	SPIB
Select Structural		2,930	3,370	3,670	1,800,000	
Non-Dense Select Structural		2,700	3,110	3,380	1,700,000	
No. 1 Dense		2,010	2,310	2,520	1,800,000	
No. 1		1,900	2,180	2,370	1,700,000	
No. 1 Non-Dense		1,720	1,980	2,160	1,600,000	
No. 2 Dense		1,670	1,920	2,080	1,700,000	
No. 2		1,440	1,650	1,800	1,600,000	
No. 2 Non-Dense		1,320	1,520	1,650	1,400,000	
No. 3		865	990	1,080	1,400,000	
Stud		890	1,020	1,110	1,400,000	
Dense Select Structural	2 × 8	2,820	3,240	3,520	1,900,000	
Select Structural		2,650	3,040	3,310	1,800,000	
Non-Dense Select Structural		2,420	2,780	3,020	1,700,000	
No. 1 Dense		1,900	2,180	2,370	1,800,000	
No. 1		1,730	1,980	2,160	1,700,000	
No. 1 Non-Dense		1,550	1,790	1,940	1,600,000	
No. 2 Dense		1,610	1,850	2,010	1,700,000	
No. 2		1,380	1,590	1,720	1,600,000	
No. 2 Non-Dense		1,260	1,450	1,580	1,400,000	
No. 3		805	925	1,010	1,400,000	
Dense Select Structural	2 × 10	2,470	2,840	3,090	1,900,000	
Select Structural		2,360	2,710	2,9500	1,800,000	
Non-Dense Select Structural		2,130	2,450	2,660	1,700,000	
No. 1 Dense		1,670	1,920	2,080	1,800,000	
No. 1		1,500	1,720	1,870	1,700,000	
No. 1 Non-Dense		1,380	1,590	1,730	1,600,000	
No. 2 Dense		1,380	1,590	1,730	1,700,000	
No. 2		1,210	1,390	1,510	1,600,000	
No. 2 Non-Dense		1,090	1,260	1,370	1,400,000	
No. 3		690	795	865	1,400,000	
Dense Select Structural	2 × 12	2,360	2,710	2,950	1,900,000	
Select Structural		2,190	2,510	2,730	1,800,000	
Non-Dense Select Structural		2,010	2,310	2,520	1,700,000	
No. 1 Dense		1,550	1,790	1,940	1,800,000	
No. 1		1,440	1,650	1,800	1,700,000	
No. 1 Non-Dense		1,320	1,520	1,650	1,600,000	
No. 2 Dense		1,320	1,520	1,650	1,700,000	
No. 2		1,120	1,290	1,400	1,600,000	
No. 2 Non-Dense		1,040	1,190	1,290	1,400,000	
No. 3		660	760	825	1,400,000	

(Continued)

TABLE 23-IV-V-1—VALUES FOR JOISTS AND RAFTERS—VISUALLY GRADED LUMBER—(Continued)

SPECIES AND GRADE	SIZE (inches)	DESIGN VALUE IN BENDING "F_b" psi			MODULUS OF ELASTICITY "E" psi	GRADING RULES AGENCY
		Normal Duration	Snow Loading	7-day Loading		
	× 25.4 for mm	× 0.00689 for N/mm²				
SPRUCE-PINE-FIR						
Select Structural	2 × 4	2,155	2,480	2,695	1,500,000	NLGA
No. 1/No. 2		1,510	1,735	1,885	1,400,000	
No. 3		865	990	1,080	1,200,000	
Stud		855	980	1,065	1,200,000	
Construction		1,120	1,290	1,400	1,300,000	
Standard		635	725	790	1,200,000	
Utility		290	330	360	1,100,000	
Select Structural	2 × 6	1,870	2,150	2,335	1,500,000	
No. 1/No. 2		1,310	1,505	1,635	1,400,000	
No. 3		750	860	935	1,200,000	
Stud		775	895	970	1,200,000	
Select Structural	2 × 8	1,725	1,985	2,155	1,500,000	
No. 1/No. 2		1,210	1,390	1,510	1,400,000	
No. 3		690	795	865	1,200,000	
Select Structural	2 × 10	1,580	1,820	1,975	1,500,000	
No. 1/No. 2		1,105	1,275	1,385	1,400,000	
No. 3		635	725	790	1,200,000	
Select Structural	2 × 12	1,440	1,655	1,795	1,500,000	
No. 1/No. 2		1,005	1,155	1,260	1,400,000	
No. 3		575	660	720	1,200,000	
SPRUCE-PINE-FIR (South)						
Select Structural	2 × 4	2,245	2,580	2,805	1,300,000	NELMA NSLB WCLIB WWPA
No. 1		1,465	1,685	1,835	1,200,000	
No. 2		1,295	1,490	1,615	1,100,000	
No. 3		735	845	915	1,000,000	
Stud		725	835	910	1,000,000	
Construction		980	1,125	1,220	1,000,000	
Standard		545	630	685	900,000	
Utility		260	300	325	900,000	
Select Structural	2 × 6	1,945	2,235	2,430	1,300,000	
No. 1		1,270	1,460	1,590	1,200,000	
No. 2		1,120	1,290	1,400	1,100,000	
No. 3		635	730	795	1,000,000	
Stud		660	760	825	1,000,000	
Select Structural	2 × 8	1,795	2,065	2,245	1,300,000	
No. 1		1,175	1,350	1,465	1,200,000	
No. 2		1,035	1,190	1,295	1,100,000	
No. 3		585	675	735	1,000,000	
Select Structural	2 × 10	1,645	1,890	2,055	1,300,000	
No. 1		1,075	1,235	1,345	1,200,000	
No. 2		950	1,090	1,185	1,100,000	
No. 3		540	620	670	1,000,000	
Select Structural	2 × 12	1,495	1,720	1,870	1,300,000	
No. 1		980	1,125	1,220	1,200,000	
No. 2		865	990	1,080	1,100,000	
No. 3		490	560	610	1,000,000	
WESTERN CEDARS						
Select Structural	2 × 4	1,725	1,985	2,155	1,100,000	WCLIB WWPA
No. 1		1,250	1,440	1,565	1,000,000	
No. 2		1,210	1,390	1,510	1,000,000	
No. 3		690	795	865	900,000	
Stud		695	800	870	900,000	
Construction		920	1,060	1,150	900,000	
Standard		520	595	645	800,000	
Utility		260	300	325	800,000	

(Continued)

TABLE 23-IV-V-1—VALUES FOR JOISTS AND RAFTERS—VISUALLY GRADED LUMBER—(Continued)

SPECIES AND GRADE	SIZE (inches)	DESIGN VALUE IN BENDING "F_b" psi			MODULUS OF ELASTICITY "E" psi	GRADING RULES AGENCY
		Normal Duration	Snow Loading	7-day Loading		
	× 25.4 for mm	× 0.00689 for N/mm²				
WESTERN CEDARS—(continued)						
Select Structural	2 × 6	1,495	1,720	1,870	1,100,000	WCLIB WWPA
No. 1		1,085	1,245	1,355	1,000,000	
No. 2		1,045	1,205	1,310	1,000,000	
No. 3		600	690	750	900,000	
Stud		635	725	790	900,000	
Select Structural	2 × 8	1,380	1,585	1,725	1,100,000	
No. 1		1,000	1,150	1,250	1,000,000	
No. 2		965	1,110	1,210	1,000,000	
No. 3		550	635	690	900,000	
Select Structural	2 × 10	1,265	1,455	1,580	1,100,000	
No. 1		915	1,055	1,145	1,000,000	
No. 2		885	1,020	1,105	1,000,000	
No. 3		505	580	635	900,000	
Select Structural	2 × 12	1,150	1,325	1,440	1,100,000	
No. 1		835	960	1,040	1,000,000	
No. 2		805	925	1,005	1,000,000	
No. 3		460	530	575	900,000	
WESTERN WOODS						
Select Structural	2 × 4	1,510	1,735	1,885	1,200,000	WCLIB WWPA
No. 1		1,120	1,290	1,400	1,100,000	
No. 2		1,120	1,290	1,400	1,000,000	
No. 3		645	745	810	900,000	
Stud		635	725	790	900,000	
Construction		835	960	1,040	1,000,000	
Standard		460	530	575	900,000	
Utility		230	265	290	800,000	
Select Structural	2 × 6	1,310	1,505	1,635	1,200,000	
No. 1		970	1,120	1,215	1,100,000	
No. 2		970	1,120	1,215	1,000,000	
No. 3		560	645	700	900,000	
Stud		575	660	720	900,000	
Select Structural	2 × 8	1,210	1,390	1,510	1,200,000	
No. 1		895	1,030	1,120	1,100,000	
No. 2		895	1,030	1,120	1,000,000	
No. 3		520	595	645	900,000	
Select Structural	2 × 10	1,105	1,275	1,385	1,200,000	
No. 1		820	945	1,030	1,100,000	
No. 2		820	945	1,030	1,000,000	
No. 3		475	545	595	900,000	
Select Structural	2 × 12	1,005	1,155	1,260	1,200,000	
No. 1		750	860	935	1,100,000	
No. 2		750	860	935	1,000,000	
No. 3		430	495	540	900,000	
WHITE OAK						
Select Structural	2 × 4	2,070	2,380	2,590	1,100,000	NELMA
No. 1		1,510	1,735	1,885	1,000,000	
No. 2		1,465	1,685	1,835	900,000	
No. 3		820	940	1,025	800,000	
Stud		820	945	1,030	800,000	
Construction		1,095	1,255	1,365	900,000	
Standard		605	695	755	800,000	
Utility		290	330	360	800,000	

(Continued)

TABLE 23-IV-V-1—VALUES FOR JOISTS AND RAFTERS—VISUALLY GRADED LUMBER—(Continued)

SPECIES AND GRADE	SIZE (inches)	DESIGN VALUE IN BENDING "F_b" psi			MODULUS OF ELASTICITY "E" psi	GRADING RULES AGENCY
		Normal Duration	Snow Loading	7-day Loading		
	× 25.4 for mm	× 0.00689 for N/mm²				
WHITE OAK—(continued)						
Select Structural	2 × 6	1,795	2,065	2,245	1,100,000	NELMA
No. 1		1,310	1,505	1,635	1,000,000	
No. 2		1,270	1,460	1,590	900,000	
No. 3		710	815	890	800,000	
Stud		750	860	935	800,000	
Select Structural	2 × 8	1,655	1,905	2,070	1,100,000	
No. 1		1,210	1,390	1,510	1,000,000	
No. 2		1,175	1,350	1,465	900,000	
No. 3		655	755	820	800,000	
Select Structural	2 × 10	1,520	1,745	1,900	1,100,000	
No. 1		1,105	1,275	1,385	1,000,000	
No. 2		1,075	1,235	1,345	900,000	
No. 3		600	690	750	800,000	
Select Structural	2 × 12	1,380	1,585	1,725	1,100,000	
No. 1		1,005	1,155	1,260	1,000,000	
No. 2		980	1,125	1,220	900,000	
No. 3		545	630	685	800,000	
YELLOW POPLAR						
Select Structural	2 × 4	1,725	1,985	2,155	1,500,000	NSLB
No. 1		1,250	1,440	1,565	1,400,000	
No. 2		1,210	1,390	1,510	1,300,000	
No. 3		690	795	865	1,200,000	
Stud		695	800	870	1,200,000	
Construction		920	1,060	1,150	1,300,000	
Standard		520	595	645	1,100,000	
Utility		230	265	290	1,100,000	
Select Structural	2 × 6	1,495	1,720	1,870	1,500,000	
No. 1		1,085	1,245	1,355	1,400,000	
No. 2		1,045	1,205	1,310	1,300,000	
No. 3		600	690	750	1,200,000	
Stud		635	725	790	1,200,000	
Select Structural	2 × 8	1,380	1,585	1,725	1,500,000	
No. 1		1,000	1,150	1,250	1,400,000	
No. 2		965	1,110	1,210	1,300,000	
No. 3		550	635	690	1,200,000	
Select Structural	2 × 10	1,265	1,455	1,580	1,500,000	
No. 1		915	1,055	1,145	1,400,000	
No. 2		885	1,020	1,105	1,300,000	
No. 3		505	580	635	1,200,000	
Select Structural	2 × 12	1,150	1,325	1,440	1,500,000	
No. 1		835	960	1,040	1,400,000	
No. 2		805	925	1,005	1,300,000	
No. 3		460	530	575	1,200,000	

TABLE 23-IV-V-2—VALUES FOR JOISTS AND RAFTERS—MECHANICALLY GRADED LUMBER
For use in Tables 23-V-J-1 through 23-V-R-12 and Division V only.

GRADE DESIGNATION	SIZE (inches)	DESIGN VALUE IN BENDING "F_b" psi			MODULUS OF ELASTICITY "E" psi	GRADING RULES AGENCIES
		Normal Duration	Snow Loading	7-day Loading		
	× 25.4 for mm	× 0.00689 for N/mm²				
MACHINE STRESS RATED (MSR) LUMBER						
900f-1.0E	2 × 4 and wider	1,040	1,190	1,290	1,000,000	WCLIB,WWPA
1200f-1.2E		1,380	1,590	1,730	1,200,000	NLGA,SPIB,WCLIB,WWPA
1350f-1.3E		1,550	1,790	1,940	1,300,000	SPIB,WCLIB,WWPA
1450f-1.3E		1,670	1,920	2,080	1,300,000	NLGA,WCLIB,WWPA
1500f-1.3E		1,730	1,980	2,160	1,300,000	SPIB
1500f-1.4E		1,730	1,980	2,160	1,400,000	NLGA,SPIB,WCLIB,WWPA
1650f-1.4E		1,900	2,180	2,370	1,400,000	SPIB
1650f-1.5E		1,900	2,180	2,370	1,500,000	NLGA,SPIB,WCLIB,WWPA
1800f-1.6E		2,070	2,380	2,590	1,600,000	NLGA,SPIB,WCLIB,WWPA
1950f-1.5E		2,240	2,580	2,800	1,500,000	SPIB
1950f-1.7E		2,240	2,580	2,800	1,700,000	NLGA,SPIB,WWPA
2100f-1.8E		2,420	2,780	3,020	1,800,000	NLGA,SPIB,WCLIB,WWPA
2250f-1.6E		2,590	2,980	3,230	1,600,000	SPIB
2250f-1.9E		2,590	2,980	3,230	1,900,000	NLGA,SPIB,WWPA
2400f-1.7E		2,760	3,170	3,450	1,700,000	SPIB
2400f-2.0E		2,760	3,170	3,450	2,000,000	NLGA,SPIB,WCLIB,WWPA
2550f-2.1E		2,930	3,370	3,670	2,100,000	NLGA,SPIB,WWPA
2700f-2.2E		3,110	3,570	3,880	2,200,000	NLGA,SPIB,WCLIB,WWPA
2850f-2.3E		3,280	3,770	4,100	2,300,000	SPIB,WWPA
3000f-2.4E		3,450	3,970	4,310	2,400,000	NLGA,SPIB
3150f-2.5E		3,620	4,170	4,530	2,500,000	SPIB
3300f-2.6E		3,800	4,360	4,740	2,600,000	SPIB
900f-1.2E	2 × 6 and wider	1,040	1,190	1,290	1,200,000	NLGA,WCLIB
1200f-1.5E		1,380	1,590	1,730	1,500,000	NLGA,WCLIB
1350f-1.8E		1,550	1,790	1,940	1,800,000	NLGA
1500f-1.8E		1,730	1,980	2,160	1,800,000	WCLIB
1800f-2.1E		2,070	2,380	2,590	2,100,000	NLGA,WCLIB
MACHINE EVALUATED LUMBER (MEL)						
M-10	2 × 4 and wider	1,610	1,850	2,010	1,200,000	SPIB
M-11		1,780	2,050	2,230	1,500,000	
M-12		1,840	2,120	2,300	1,600,000	
M-13		1,840	2,120	2,300	1,400,000	
M-14		2,070	2,380	2,590	1,700,000	
M-15		2,070	2,380	2,590	1,500,000	
M-16		2,070	2,380	2,590	1,500,000	
M-17		2,240	2,580	2,800	1,700,000	
M-18		2,300	2,650	2,880	1,800,000	
M-19		2,300	2,650	2,880	1,600,000	
M-20		2,300	2,650	2,880	1,900,000	
M-21		2,650	3,040	3,310	1,900,000	
M-22		2,700	3,110	3,380	1,700,000	
M-23		2,760	3,170	3,450	1,800,000	
M-24		3,110	3,570	3,880	1,900,000	
M-25		3,160	3,640	3,950	2,200,000	
M-26		3,220	3,700	4,030	2,000,000	
M-27		3,450	3,970	4,310	2,100,000	

The note to Table 23-IV-V-1 applies also to mechanically graded lumber.

TABLE 25-B[1]—TYPES OF LATH—MAXIMUM SPACING OF SUPPORTS

TYPE OF LATH[2]		MINIMUM WEIGHT (per square yard) (× 0.38 for kg/m²) GAGE AND MESH SIZE (× 25.4 for mm)	VERTICAL (inches) × 25.4 for mm			HORIZONTAL (inches) × 25.4 for mm	
			Wood	Metal: Solid Plaster Partitions	Metal: Other	Wood or Concrete	Metal
1. Expanded metal lath (diamond mesh)		2.5 3.4	16[3] 16[3]	16[3] 16[3]	12 16	12 16	12 16
2. Flat rib expanded metal lath		2.75 3.4	16 19	16 24	16 19	16 19	16 19
3. Stucco mesh expanded metal lath		1.8 and 3.6	16[4]	—	—	—	—
4. 3/8″ (9.5 mm) rib expanded metal lath		3.4 4.0	24 24	24[5] 24[5]	24 24	24 24	24 24
5. Sheet lath		4.5	24	[5]	24	24	24
6. Wire fabric lath	Welded	1.95 pounds, 0.120 inch (No. 11 B.W. gage), 2″ x 2″ 1.16 pounds, 0.065 inch (No. 16 B.W. gage), 2″ x 2″ 1.4 pounds, 0.049 inch (No. 18 B.W. gage), 1″ x 1″[6]	24 16 16[4]	24 16 —	24 16 —	24 16 —	24 16 —
	Woven	1.1 pounds, 0.049 inch (No. 18 B.W. gage), 1½″ hexagonal[6] 1.4 pounds, 0.058 inch (No. 17 B.W. gage), 1½″ hexagonal[6] 1.4 pounds, 0.049 inch (No. 18 B.W. gage), 1″ hexagonal[6]	24 24 24	16 16 16	16 16 16	24 24 24	16 16 16
7. 3/8″ (9.5 mm) gypsum lath (plain)			16	—	16[7]	16	16
8. 1/2″ (12.7 mm) gypsum lath (plain)			24	—	24	24	24

[1]For fire-resistive construction, see Tables 7-A, 7-B and 7-C. For shear-resisting elements, see Table 25-I.

[2]Metal lath and wire fabric lath used as reinforcement for cement plaster shall be furred out away from vertical supports at least 1/4 inch (6.4 mm). Self-furring lath meets furring requirements.

EXCEPTION: Furring of expanded metal lath is not required on supports having a bearing surface width of 1 5/8 inches (41 mm) or less.

[3]Span may be increased to 24 inches (610 mm) with self-furred metal lath over solid sheathing assemblies approved for this use.

[4]Wire backing required on open vertical frame construction except under expanded metal lath and paperbacked wire fabric lath.

[5]May be used for studless solid partitions.

[6]Woven wire or welded wire fabric lath not to be used as base for gypsum plaster without absorbent paperbacking or slot-perforated separator.

[7]Span may be increased to 24 inches (610 mm) on vertical screw or approved nailable assemblies.

TABLE 25-C—TYPES OF LATH—ATTACHMENT TO WOOD AND METAL[1] SUPPORTS

TYPE OF LATH	NAILS[2,3]			SCREWS[3,4]		STAPLES[3,5] Round or Flattened Wire				
	Type and Size	Maximum Spacing[6]		Maximum Spacing[6]		Wire Gage No.			Maximum Spacing[6]	
		Vertical	Horizontal	Vertical	Horizontal		Crown	Leg	Vertical	Horizontal
		(inches)					(inches)			
	× 25.4 for mm						× 25.4 for mm			
1. Diamond mesh expanded metal lath and flat rib metal lath	4d blued smooth box 1 1/2″[7] No. 14 gage 7/32″ head (clinched)[8] 1″ No. 11 gage 7/16″ head, barbed 1 1/2″ No. 11 gage 7/16″ head, barbed	6 6 6	— — 6	6	6	16	3/4	7/8	6	6
2. 3/8″ (9.5 mm) rib metal lath and sheet lath	1 1/2″ No. 11 gage 7/16″ head, barbed	6	6	6	6	16	3/4	1 1/4	At ribs	At ribs
3. 3/4″ (19.1 mm) rib metal lath	4d common 1 1/2″ No. 12 1/2 gage 1/4″ head 2″ No. 11 gage 7/16″ head, barbed	At ribs	— At ribs	At ribs	At ribs	16	3/4	1 5/8	At ribs	At ribs
4. Wire fabric lath[9]	4d blued smooth box (clinched)[8] 1″ No. 11 gage 7/16″ head, barbed	6 6	— —	6	6	16	3/4	7/8	6	6
	1 1/2″ No. 11 gage 7/16″ head, barbed 1 1/4″ No. 12 gage 3/8″ head, furring 1″ No. 12 gage 3/8″ head	6 6 6	6 6			16	7/16[9]	7/8	6	6
5. 3/8″ (9.5 mm) gypsum lath	1 1/8″ No. 13 gage 19/64″ head, blued	8[10]	8[10]	8[10]	8[10]	16	3/4	7/8[11]	8[10]	8[10]
6. 1/2″ (12.7 mm) gypsum lath	1 1/4″ No. 13 gage 19/64″ head, blued	8	8[10] 6[7]	8[10]	8[10] 6[7]	16	3/4	1 1/8[11]	8[10]	8[10] 6[7]

[1]Metal lath, wire lath, wire fabric lath and metal accessories shall conform to approved standards.
[2]For nailable nonload-bearing metal supports, use annular threaded nails or approved staples.
[3]For fire-resistive construction, see Tables 7-B and 7-C. For shear-resisting elements, see Table 25-I. Approved wire and sheet metal attachment clips may be used.
[4]Screws shall be an approved type long enough to penetrate into wood framing not less than 5/8 inch (15.9 mm) and through metal supports adaptable for screw attachment not less than 1/4 inch (6.4 mm).
[5]With chisel or divergent points.
[6]Maximum spacing of attachments from longitudinal edges shall not exceed 2 inches (51 mm).
[7]Supports spaced 24 inches (610 mm) on center. Four attachments per 16-inch-wide (406 mm) lath per bearing. Five attachments per 24-inch-wide (610 mm) lath per bearing.
[8]For interiors only.
[9]Attach self-furring wire fabric lath to supports at furring device.
[10]Three attachments per 16-inch-wide (406.4 mm) lath per bearing. Four attachments per 24-inch-wide (610 mm) lath per bearing.
[11]When lath and stripping are stapled simultaneously, increase leg length of staple 1/8 inch (3.2 mm).

TABLE 25-D—THICKNESS OF PLASTER[1]

PLASTER BASE	FINISHED THICKNESS OF PLASTER FROM FACE OF LATH, MASONRY, CONCRETE × 25.4 for mm	
	Gypsum Plaster	Portland Cement Plaster
1. Expanded metal lath	5/8″ minimum[2]	5/8″ minimum[2]
2. Wire fabric lath	5/8″ minimum[2]	3/4″ minimum (interior)[3] 7/8″ minimum (exterior)[3]
3. Gypsum lath	1/2″ minimum	
4. Masonry walls[4]	1/2″ minimum	1/2″ minimum
5. Monolithic concrete walls[4,5]	5/8″ maximum[6]	7/8″ maximum[6]
6. Monolithic concrete ceilings[4,5]	3/8″ maximum[6,7,8]	1/2″ maximum[7,8]

[1]For fire-resistive construction, see Tables 7-A, 7-B and 7-C.
[2]When measured from back plane of expanded metal lath, exclusive of ribs, or self-furring lath, plaster thickness shall be 3/4 inch (19 mm) minimum.
[3]When measured from face of support or backing.
[4]Because masonry and concrete surfaces may vary in plane, thickness of plaster need not be uniform.
[5]When applied over a liquid bonding agent, finish coat may be applied directly to concrete surface.
[6]An approved skim-coat plaster 1/16 inch (1.6 mm) thick may be applied directly to concrete.
[7]On concrete ceilings, where the base coat plaster thickness exceeds the maximum thickness shown, metal lath or wire fabric lath shall be attached to the concrete.
[8]Approved acoustical plaster may be applied directly to concrete, or over base coat plaster, beyond the maximum plaster thickness shown.

TABLE 25-E—GYPSUM PLASTER PROPORTIONS[1]

NUMBER	COAT	PLASTER BASE OR LATH	MAXIMUM VOLUME AGGREGATE PER 100 POUNDS (45.4 kg) NEAT PLASTER[2,3] (cubic feet) × 0.028 for m^3	
			Damp Loose Sand[4]	Perlite or Vermiculite[4]
1. Two-coat work	Base coat	Gypsum lath	2 1/2	2
	Base coat	Masonry	3	3
2. Three-coat work	First coat	Lath	2[5]	2
	Second coat	Lath	3[5]	2[6]
	First and second coats	Masonry	3	3

[1]Wood-fibered gypsum plaster may be mixed in the proportions of 100 pounds (45.4 kg) of gypsum to not more than 1 cubic foot (0.028 m^3) of sand where applied on masonry or concrete.

[2]For fire-resistive construction, see Tables 7-A, 7-B and 7-C.

[3]When determining the amount of aggregate in set plaster, a tolerance of 10 percent shall be allowed.

[4]Combinations of sand and lightweight aggregate may be used, provided the volume and weight relationship of the combined aggregate to gypsum plaster is maintained.

[5]If used for both first and second coats, the volume of aggregate may be 2 1/2 cubic feet (0.07 m^3).

[6]Where plaster is 1 inch (25 mm) or more in total thickness, the proportions for the second coat may be increased to 3 cubic feet (0.08 m^3).

TABLE 25-F—CEMENT PLASTERS[1]

PORTLAND CEMENT PLASTER						
Coat	Volume Cement	Maximum Weight (or Volume) Lime per Volume Cement	Maximum Volume Sand per Combined Volumes Cement and Lime[2]	Approximate Minimum Thickness[3] × 25.4 for mm	Minimum Period Moist Curing	Minimum Interval between Coats
First	1	20 lbs. (9.07 kg)	4	3/8″[4]	48 hours[5]	48 hours[6]
Second	1	20 lbs. (9.07 kg)	5	1st and 2nd coats total 3/4″	48 hours	7 days[7]
Finish	1	1[8]	3	1st, 2nd and finish coats 7/8″	—	7
PORTLAND CEMENT-LIME PLASTER[9]						
Coat	Volume Cement	Maximum Volume Lime per Volume Cement	Maximum Volume Sand per Combined Volumes Cement and Lime[3]	Approximate Minimum Thickness[3] × 25.4 for mm	Minimum Period Moist Curing	Minimum Interval between Coats
First	1	1	4	3/8″[4]	48 hours[5]	48 hours[6]
Second	1	1	4 1/2	1st and 2nd coats total 3/4″	48 hours	7 days[7]
Finish	1	1[8]	3	1st, 2nd and finish coats 7/8″	—	7
PLASTIC CEMENT PLASTER[9]						
Coat	Volume Cement	Maximum Weight (or Volume) Lime per Volume Cement	Maximum Volume Sand per Volume Cement[2]	Approximate Minimum Thickness[3] × 25.4 for mm	Minimum Period Moist Curing	Minimum Interval between Coats
First	1	—	4	3/8″[4]	48 hours[5]	48 hours[6]
Second	1	—	5	1st and 2nd coats total 3/4″	48 hours	7 days[7]
Finish	1	—	3	1st, 2nd and finish coats 7/8″	—	7

[1]Exposed aggregate plaster shall be applied in accordance with Section 2509. Minimum overall thickness shall be 3/4 inch (19 mm).

[2]When determining the amount of sand in set plaster, a tolerance of 10 percent may be allowed.

[3]See Table 25-D.

[4]Measured from face of support or backing to crest of scored plaster.

[5]See Section 2507.3.3.

[6]Twenty-four-hour minimum interval between coats of interior cement plaster. For alternate method of application, see Section 2508.6.

[7]Finish coat plaster may be applied to interior portland cement base coats after a 48-hour period.

[8]For finish coat plaster, up to an equal part of dry hydrated lime by weight (or an equivalent volume of lime putty) may be added to Types I, II and III standard portland cement.

[9]No additions of plasticizing agents shall be made.

TABLE 25-G—SINGLE-PLY GYPSUM WALLBOARD APPLIED PARALLEL (||) OR PERPENDICULAR (⊥) TO FRAMING MEMBERS

THICKNESS OF GYPSUM WALLBOARD (inch)	PLANE OF FRAMING SURFACE	MAXIMUM SPACING OF FRAMING MEMBER[1] (Center to Center) (inches)	LONG DIMENSION OF GYPSUM WALLBOARD SHEETS IN RELATION TO DIRECTION OF FRAMING MEMBERS		MAXIMUM SPACING OF FASTENERS[1] (Center to Center) (inches)		NAILS[2]—TO WOOD
× 25.4 for mm		× 25.4 for mm	||	⊥	Nails[3]	Screws[4]	× 25.4 for mm
1/2	Horizontal	16	P	P	7	12	No. 13 gage, 1 3/8″ long, 19/64″ head; 0.098″ diameter, 1 1/4″ long, annular ringed; 5d, cooler (0.086″ dia., 1 5/8″ long, 15/64″ head) or wallboard (0.086″ dia., 1 5/8″ long, 9/32″ head) nail.
		24	NP	P			
	Vertical	16	P	P	8	16	
		24	P	P		12	
5/8	Horizontal	16	P	P	7	12	No. 13 gage, 1 5/8″ long, 19/64″ head; 0.098″ diameter, 1 3/8″ long, annular ringed; 6d, cooler (0.092″ dia., 1 7/8″ long, 1/4″ head) or wallboard (0.0915″ dia., 1 7/8″ long, 19/64″ head) nail.
		24	NP	P			
	Vertical	16	P	P	8	16	
		24	P	P		12	

Nail or Screw Fastenings with Adhesives (Maximum Center to Center in Inches) × 25.4 for mm								
(Column headings as above)					End	Edges	Field	
1/2 or 5/8	Horizontal	16	P	P	16	16	24	As required for 1/2″ and 5/8″ gypsum wallboard, see above.
		24	NP	P	16	24	24	
	Vertical	24	P	P	16	24	NR	

NOTES: Horizontal refers to applications such as ceilings. Vertical refers to applications such as walls.

|| denotes parallel.

⊥ denotes perpendicular. P—Permitted. NP—Not permitted. NR—Not required.

[1] A combination of fasteners consisting of nails along the perimeter and screws in the field of the gypsum board may be used with the spacing of the fasteners shown in the table.

For fire-resistive construction, see Tables 7-B and 7-C. For shear-resisting elements, see Table 25-I.

[2] Where the metal framing has a clinching design formed to receive the nails by two edges of metal, the nails shall not be less than 5/8 inch (15.9 mm) longer than the wallboard thickness, and shall have ringed shanks. Where the metal framing has a nailing groove formed to receive the nails, the nails shall have barbed shanks or be 5d, No. 13 1/2 gage, 1 5/8 inches (41 mm) long, 15/64-inch (6.0 mm) head for 1/2-inch (12.7 mm) gypsum wallboard; 6d, No. 13 gage, 1 7/8 (48 mm) inches long, 15/64-inch (6.0 mm) head for 5/8-inch (15.9 mm) gypsum wallboard.

[3] Two nails spaced 2 inches to 2 1/2 inches (51 mm to 64 mm) apart may be used where the pairs are spaced 12 inches (305 mm) on center except around the perimeter of the sheets.

[4] Screws shall be long enough to penetrate into wood framing not less than 5/8 inch (15.9 mm) and through metal framing not less than 1/4 inch (6.4 mm).

TABLE 25-H—APPLICATION OF TWO-PLY GYPSUM WALLBOARD[1]

Thickness of Gypsum Wallboard (Each Ply) (inch)	Plane of Framing Surface	Long Dimension of Gypsum Wallboard Sheets	Maximum Spacing of Framing Members (Center to Center) (inches)	Maximum Spacing of Fasteners (Center to Center) (inches) × 25.4 for mm: Base Ply			Face Ply	
× 25.4 for mm			× 25.4 for mm	Nails[2]	Screws[3]	Staples[4]	Nails[2]	Screws[3]
FASTENERS ONLY								
3/8	Horizontal	Perpendicular only	16	16	24	16	7	12
	Vertical	Either direction	16				8	
1/2	Horizontal	Perpendicular only	24				7	
	Vertical	Either direction	24				8	
5/8	Horizontal	Perpendicular only	24				7	
	Vertical	Either direction	24				8	
FASTENERS AND ADHESIVES								
3/8 Base ply	Horizontal	Perpendicular only	16	7	12	5	Temporary nailing or shoring to comply with Section 2511.4	
	Vertical	Either direction	24	8		7		
1/2 Base ply	Horizontal	Perpendicular only	24	7		5		
	Vertical	Either direction	24	8		7		
5/8 Base ply	Horizontal	Perpendicular only	24	7		5		
	Vertical	Either direction	24	8		7		

[1] For fire-resistive construction, see Tables 7-B and 7-C. For shear-resisting elements, see Table 25-I.

[2] Nails for wood framing shall be long enough to penetrate into wood members not less than 3/4 inch (19.1 mm), and the sizes shall comply with the provisions of Table 25-G. For nails not included in Table 25-G, use the appropriate size cooler or wallboard nails. Nails for metal framing shall comply with the provisions of Table 25-G.

[3] Screws shall comply with the provisions of Table 25-G.

[4] Staples shall not be less than No. 16 gage by 3/4-inch (19.1 mm) crown width with leg length of 7/8 inch (22.2 mm), 1 1/8 inches (28.6 mm) and 1 3/8 inches (34.9 mm) for gypsum wallboard thicknesses of 3/8 inch (9.5 mm), 1/2 inch (12.7 mm) and 5/8 inch (15.9 mm), respectively.

TABLE 31-A—MINIMUM PASSAGEWAY AREAS FOR MASONRY CHIMNEYS[1]

Type of Masonry Chimney	MINIMUM CROSS-SECTIONAL AREA × 645 for mm² — Tile Lined: Round	Tile Lined: Square or Rectangle	Lined with Firebrick or Unlined
1. Residential (other than fireplaces)	50 square inches	50 square inches	85 square inches
2. Fireplace	See Figure 31-1	See Figure 31-1	1/8 of opening minimum 100 square inches
3. Low heat	50 square inches	57 square inches	135 square inches
4. Incinerator Apartment type 1 opening 2 to 6 openings 7 to 14 openings 15 or more openings	196 square inches 324 square inches 484 square inches 484 square inches plus 10 square inches for each additional opening		Not applicable

NOTE: For altitudes over 2,000 feet (610 m) above sea level, the building official shall be consulted in determining the area of the passageway.

[1]Areas for medium- and high-heat chimneys shall be determined using accepted engineering methods and as approved by the building official.

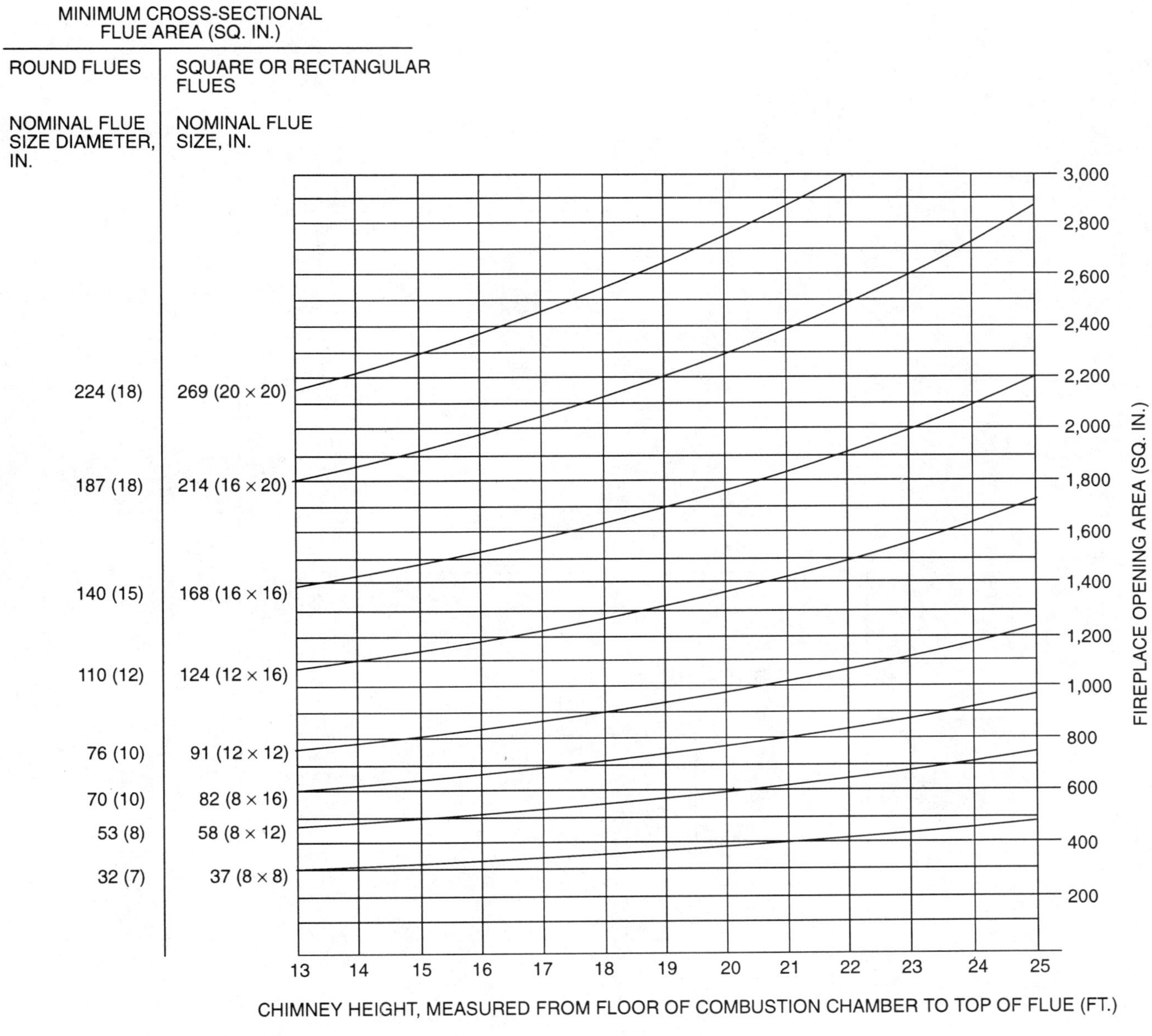

For **SI:** 1 inch = 25.4 mm, 1 square inch = 654.16 mm^2, 1 foot = 304.8 mm.

FIGURE 31-1—FLUE SIZES FOR MASONRY CHIMNEYS[1]

[1]The smaller flue area shall be utilized where the fireplace opening area and the chimney height selected intersect between flue area curves.

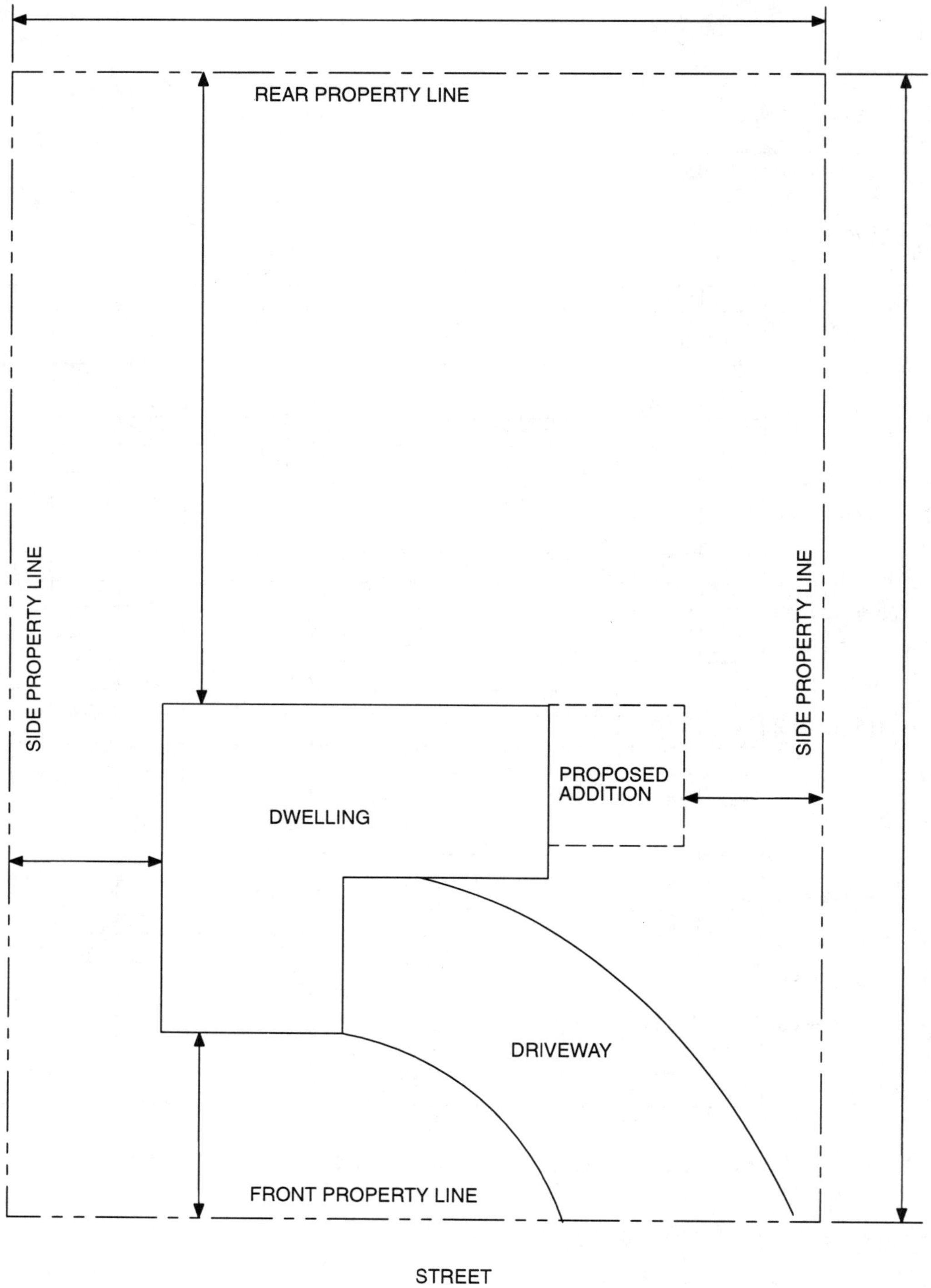

FIGURE 1—TYPICAL PLOT PLAN

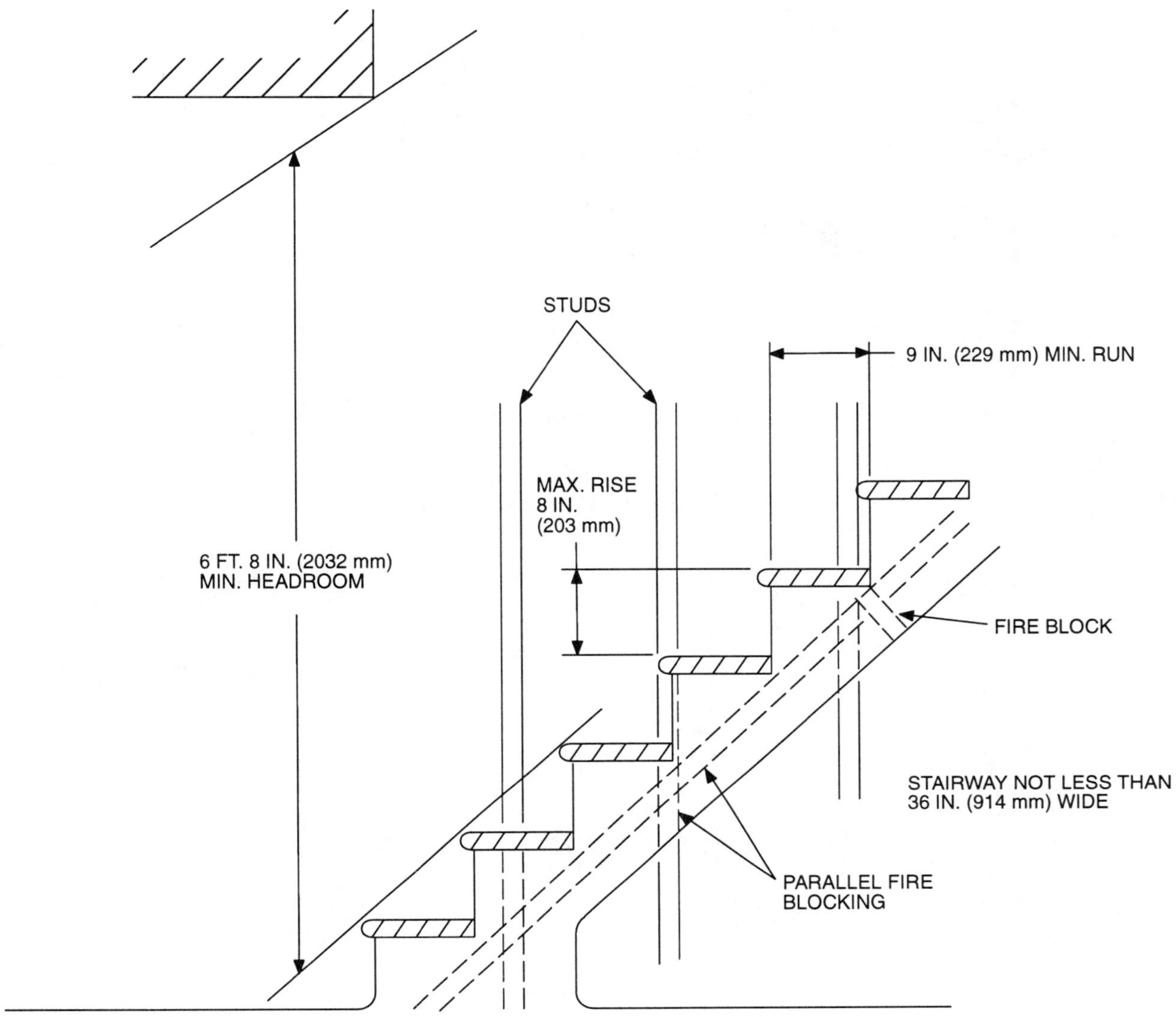

FIGURE 2—PRIVATE STAIRWAY DETAIL

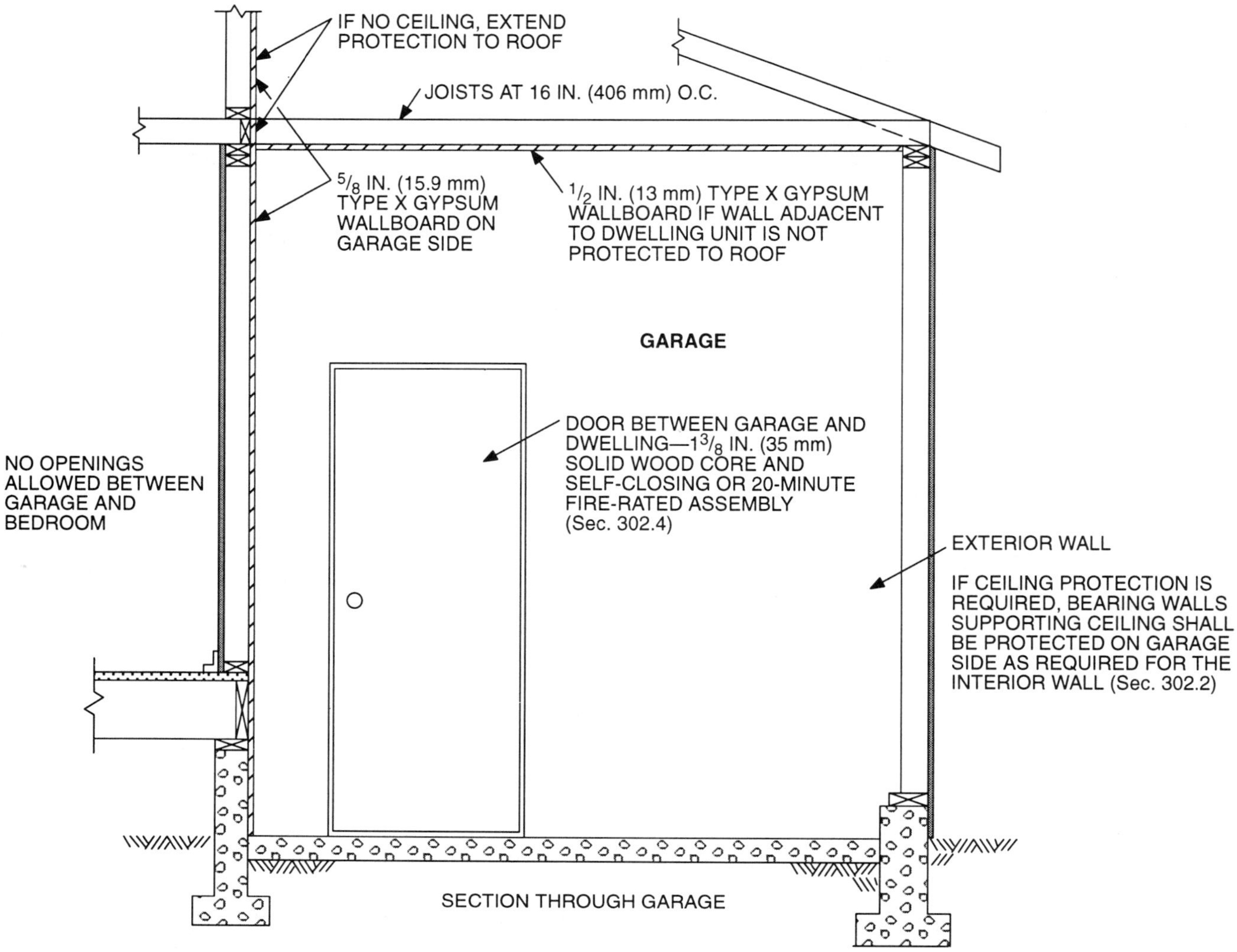

FIGURE 3—FIRE-PROTECTED WALL OF ATTACHED PRIVATE GARAGE

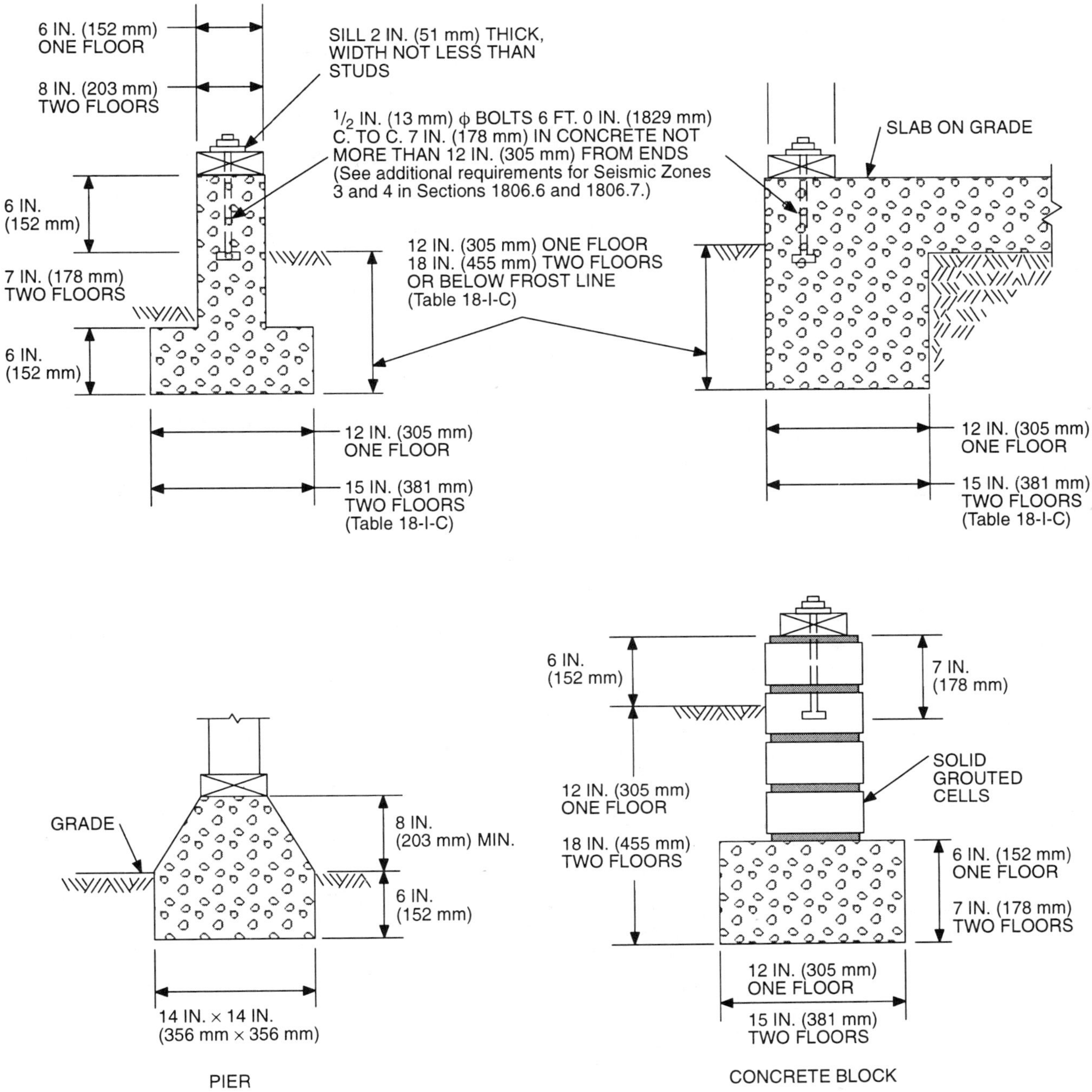

ALL FOUNDATIONS TO EXTEND INTO NATURAL
UNDISTURBED GROUND BELOW FROST LINE

FIGURE 4—FOUNDATION EXTENSION DETAIL

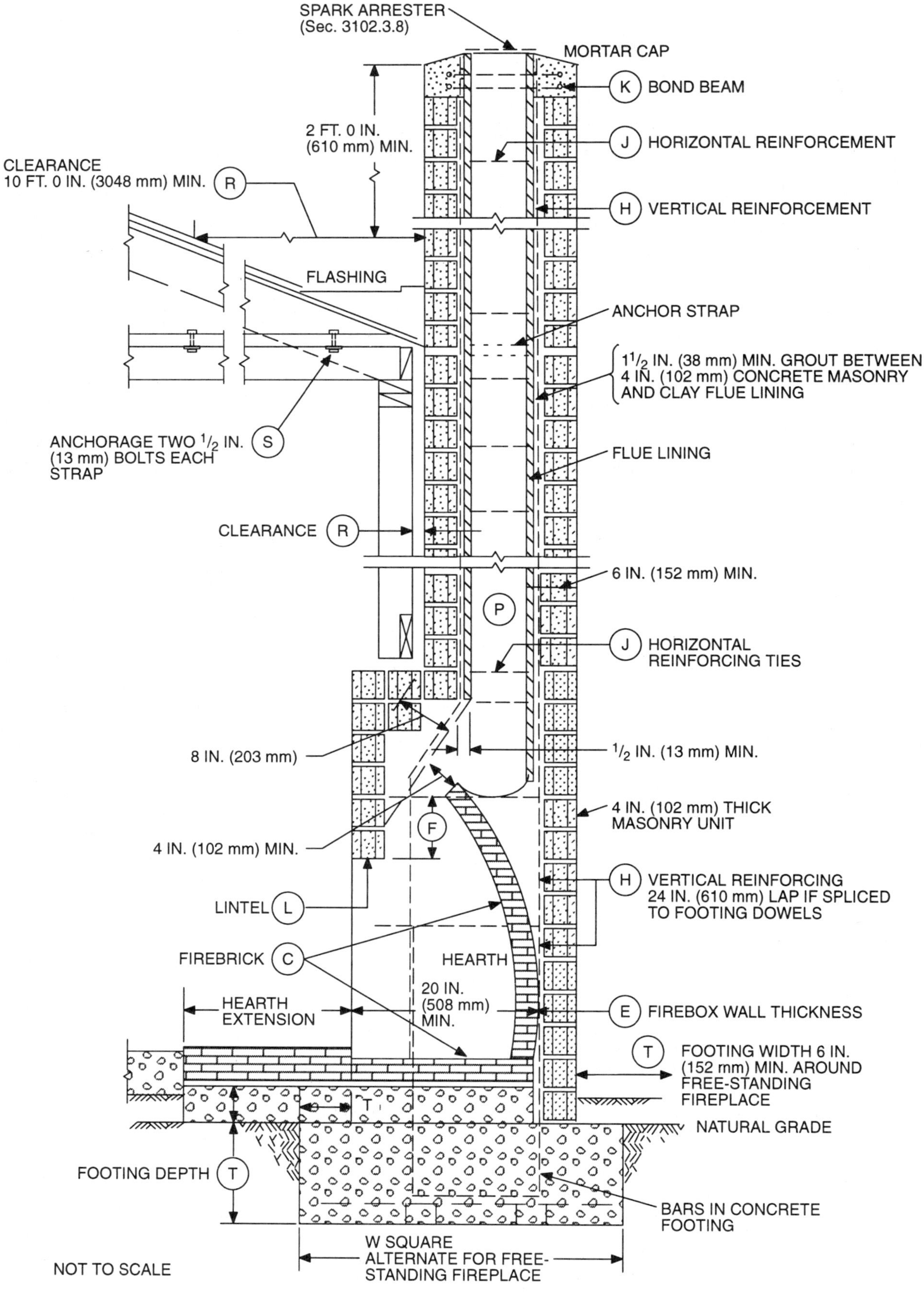

**BRICK FIREBOX AND CHIMNEY–
SECTIONAL SIDE VIEW ON CONCRETE SLAB**

SEE PAGE 67 FOR KEY LETTER REFERENCES

FIGURE 5—TYPICAL MASONRY FIREPLACE

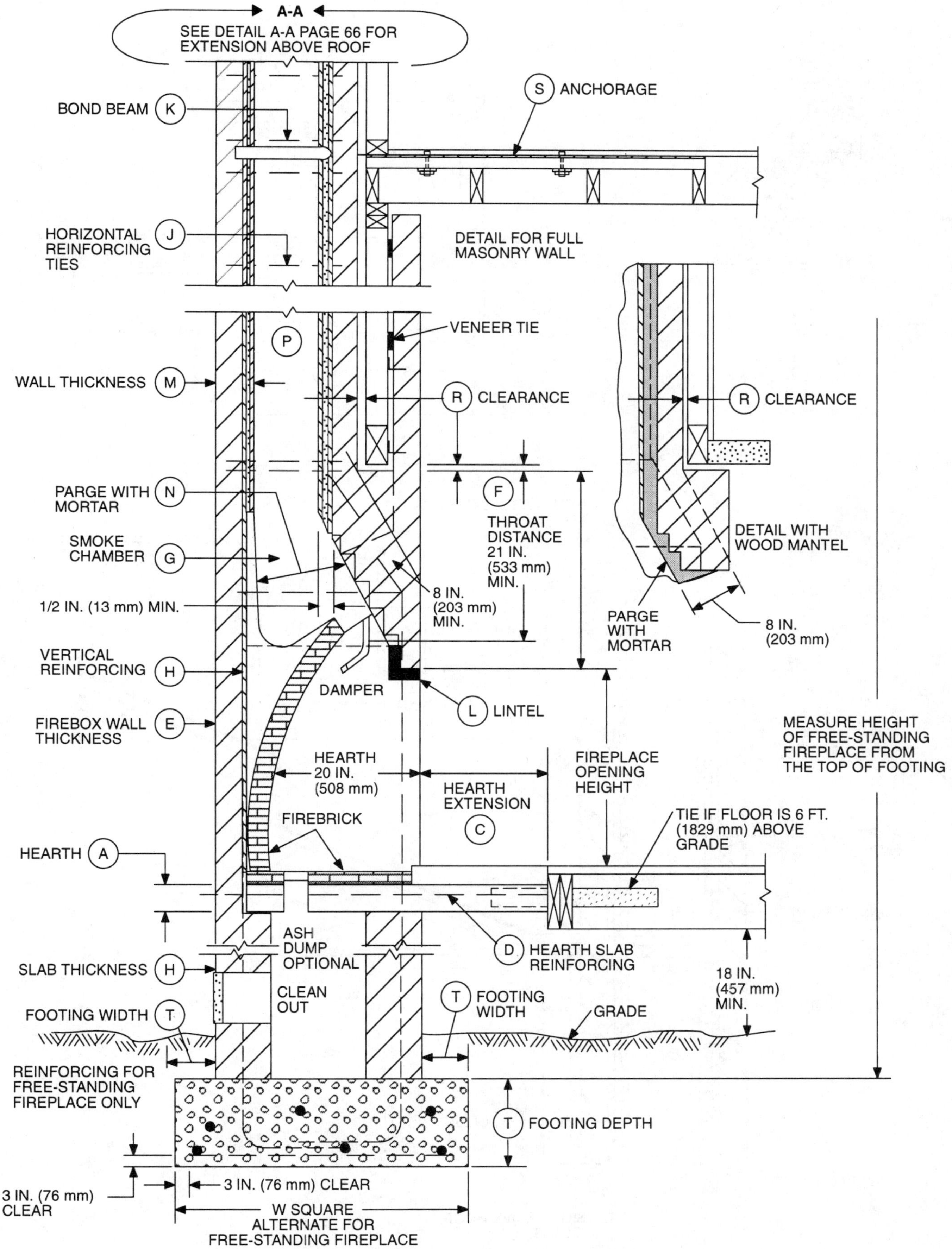

NOT TO SCALE

BRICK FIREBOX AND CHIMNEY—SECTIONAL SIDE VIEW ON WOOD FLOOR

FIGURE 5—TYPICAL MASONRY FIREPLACE—(Continued)

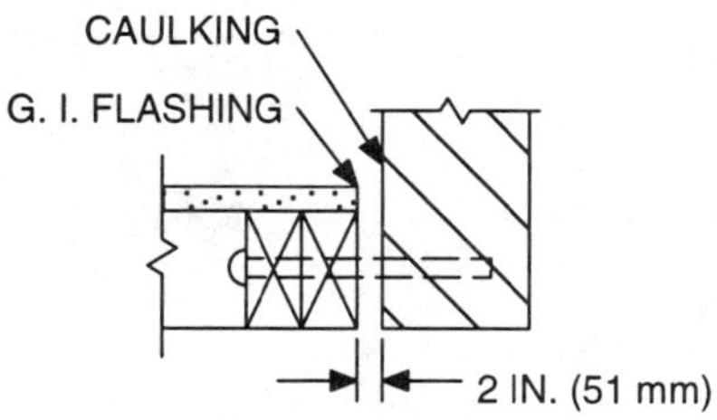

VERTICAL FLASHING DETAIL B-B

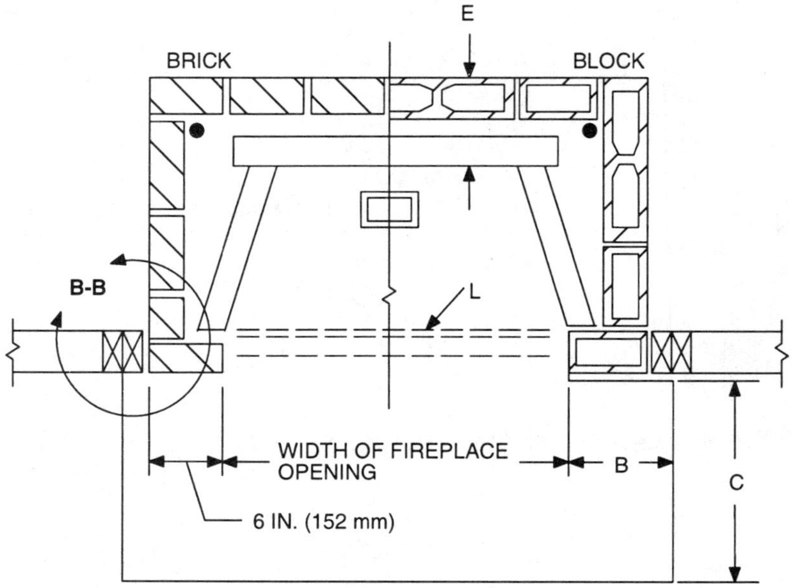

PLAN VIEW

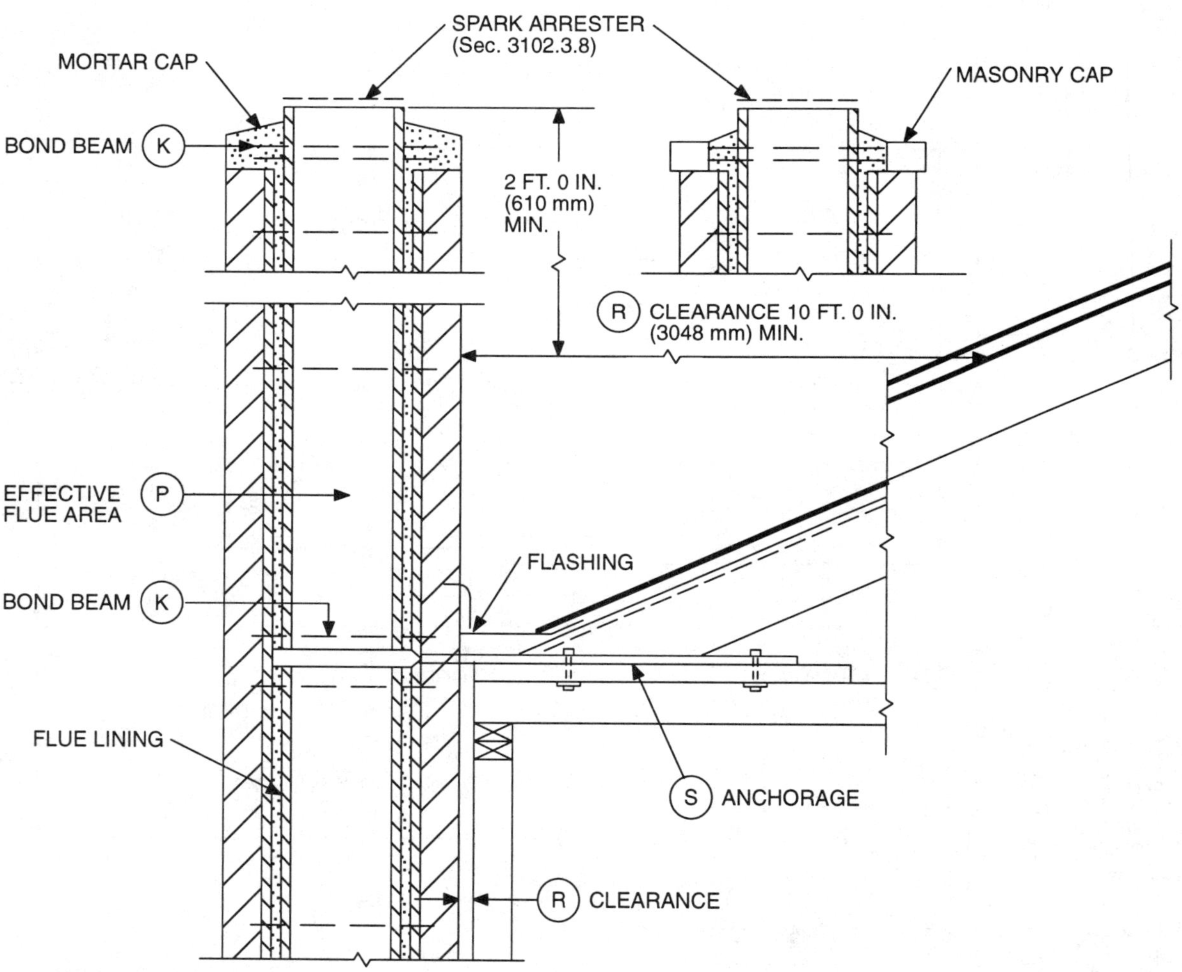

NOT TO SCALE

EXTENSION ABOVE ROOF DETAIL A-A

FIGURE 5—TYPICAL MASONRY FIREPLACE—(Continued)

UBC REQUIREMENTS FOR MASONRY FIREPLACES

ITEM	LETTER*	UNIFORM BUILDING CODE REQUIREMENTS
Hearth slab thickness	A	4″ (102 mm)
Hearth extension (each side of opening)	B	8″ (203 mm) fireplace opening < 6 sq. ft. (0.56 m^2) 12″ (305 mm) fireplace opening ≥ 6 sq. ft. (0.56 m^2)
Hearth extension (front of opening)	C	16″ (406 mm) fireplace opening < 6 sq. ft. (0.56 m^2) 20″ (508 mm) fireplace opening ≥ 6 sq. ft. (0.56 m^2)
Hearth slab reinforcing	D	Reinforced to carry its own weight and all imposed loads.
Thickness of wall of firebox	E	10″ (254 mm) common brick or 8″ (203 mm) where a firebrick lining is used. Joints in firebrick $^1/_4$″ (6 mm) max.
Distance from top of opening to throat	F	6″ (152 mm)
Smoke chamber edge of shelf Rear wall—thickness Front and sidewall—thickness	G	 6″ (152 mm) 8″ (203 mm)
Chimney Vertical reinforcing	H	Four No. 4 full-length bars for chimney up to 40″ (1016 mm) wide. Add two No. 4 bars for each additional 40″ (1016 mm) or fraction of width or each additional flue. (Seismic Zones 2, 3 and 4.)
Horizontal reinforcing	J	$^1/_4$″ (6.4 mm) ties at 18″ (457 mm) and two ties at each bend in vertical steel.
Bond beams	K	No specified requirements.
Fireplace lintel	L	Noncombustible material.
Walls with flue lining	M	Brick with grout around lining. 4″ (102 mm) min. from flue lining to outside face of chimney.
Walls with unlined flue	N	8″ (203 mm) solid masonry.
Distances between adjacent flues		4″ (102 mm)
Minimum effective flue area (based on area of fireplace opening)	P	Round lining—$^1/_{12}$ or 50 sq. in. (32 258 mm^2) min. Rectangular lining—$^1/_{10}$ or 64 sq. in. (41 290 mm^2) min. Unlined or lined with firebrick—$^1/_8$ or 100 sq. in. (64 516 mm^2) min.
Clearances Wood frame Combustible material Above roof	R	2″ (51 mm) (See Figure 8) 6″ (152 mm) min. to fireplace opening. 12″ (305 mm) from opening when material projecting more than $^1/_8$ for each 1″ (25 mm). 2′ (610 mm) at 10′ (3048 mm) (See UBC Table 31-B.)
Anchorage Strap Number Embedment into chimney Fasten to Bolts	S	 $^3/_{16}$″ × 1″ (4.8 mm by 25 mm) 2 12″ (305 mm) hooked around outer bar w/6″ (152 mm) ext. 2″ × 4″ (51 mm by 102 mm) ties crossing a min. of 4 joists Two $^1/_2$″ (13 mm) diameter
Footing Thickness Width	T	 12″ (305 mm) min. 6″ (152 mm) each side of fireplace wall

NOTE: *See figure for letter references.
Steel reinforcement shown is required in Seismic Zones 2, 3 and 4.
See "Chimneys, Fireplaces and Barbecues" for additional information.

FIGURE 5—TYPICAL MASONRY FIREPLACE—(Continued)

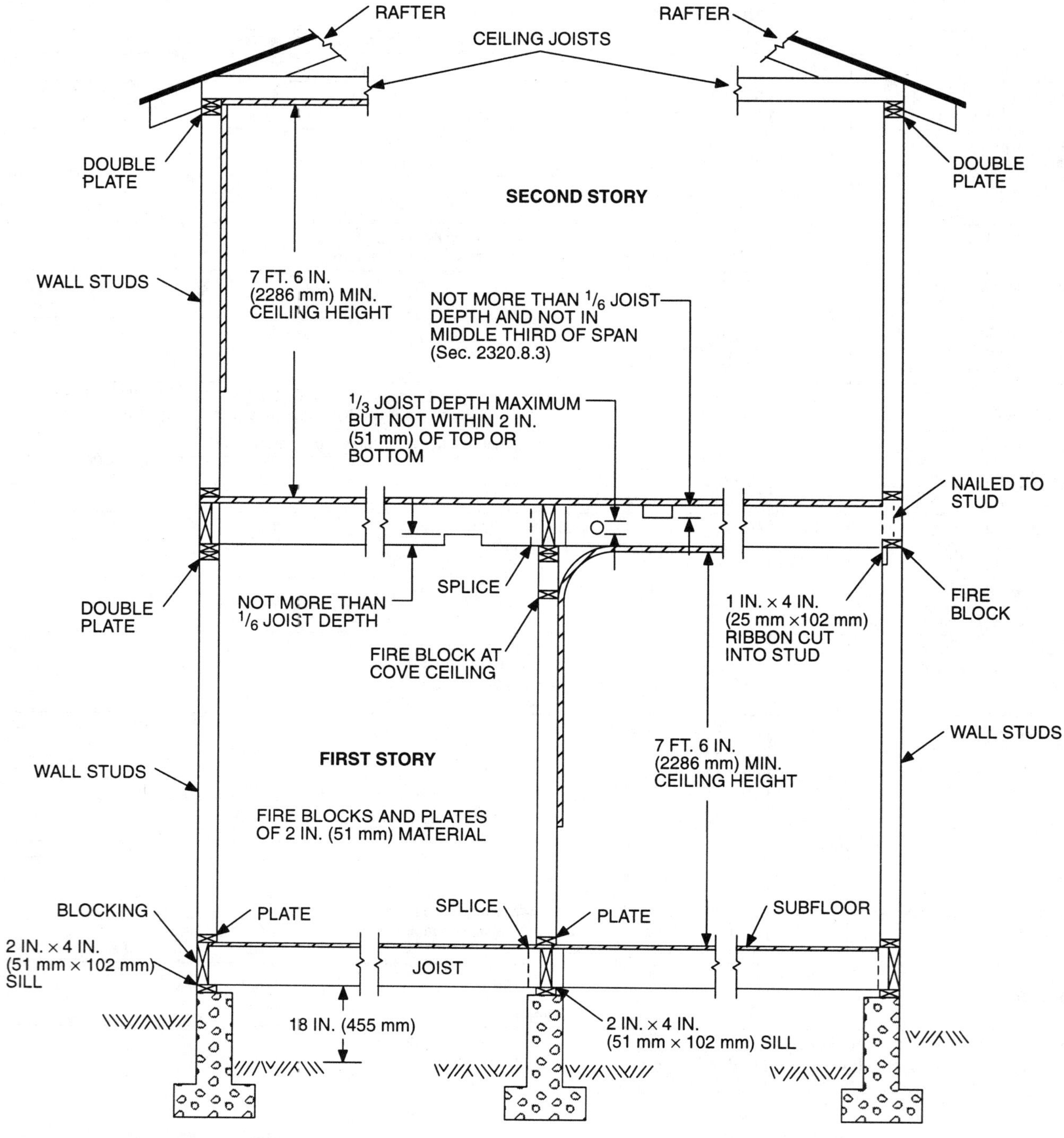

FIGURE 6—FRAMING SECTION

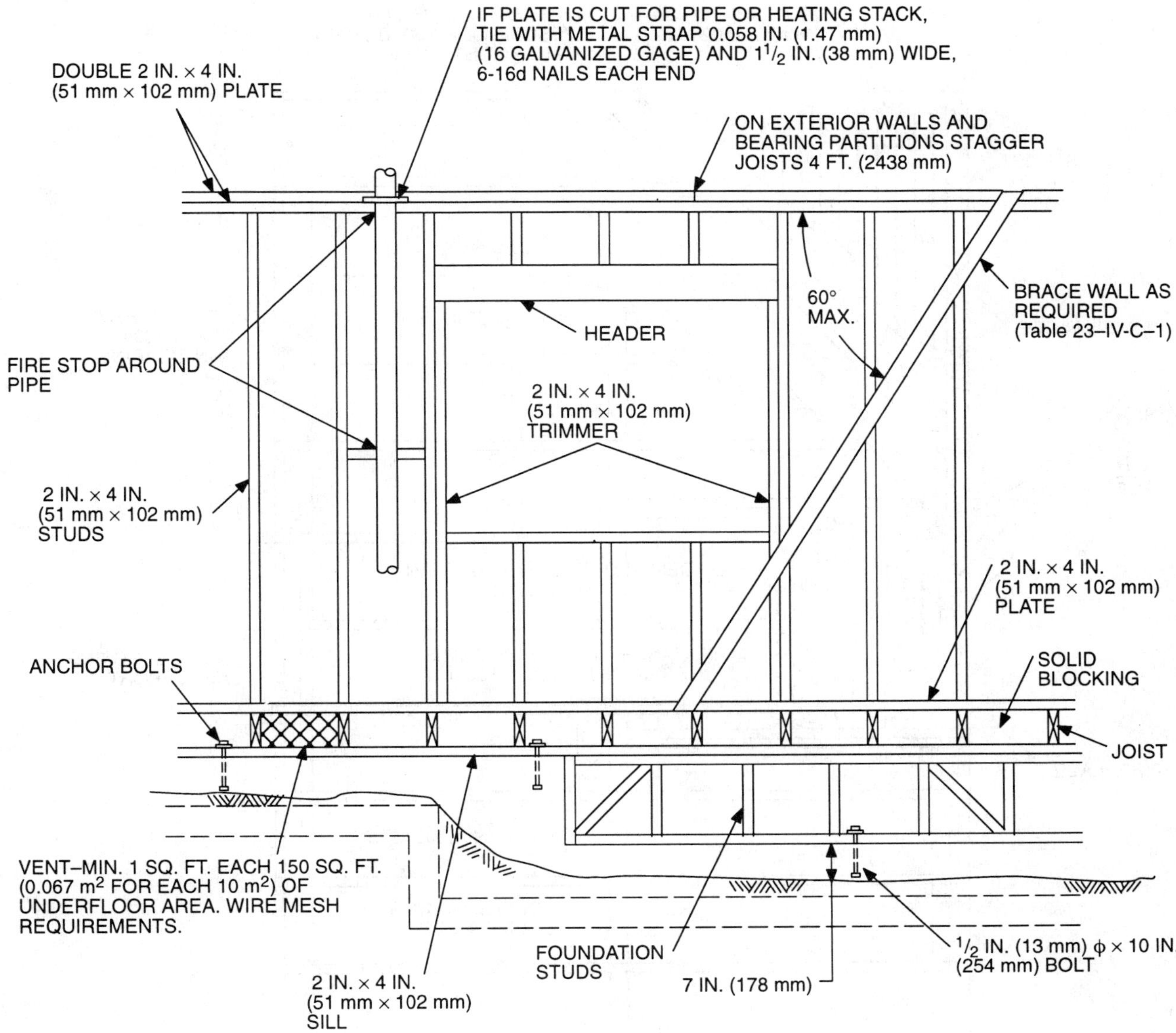

WALL FRAMING ABOVE FOUNDATION

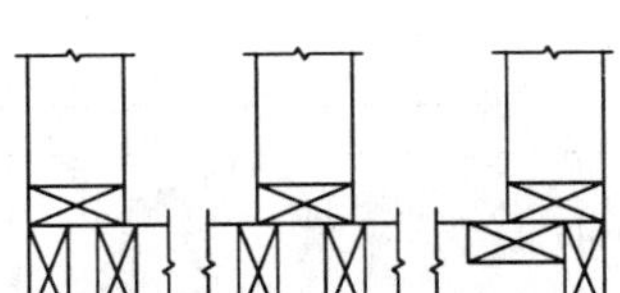

CORNER STUDS

FIGURE 7—WALL FRAMING DETAIL

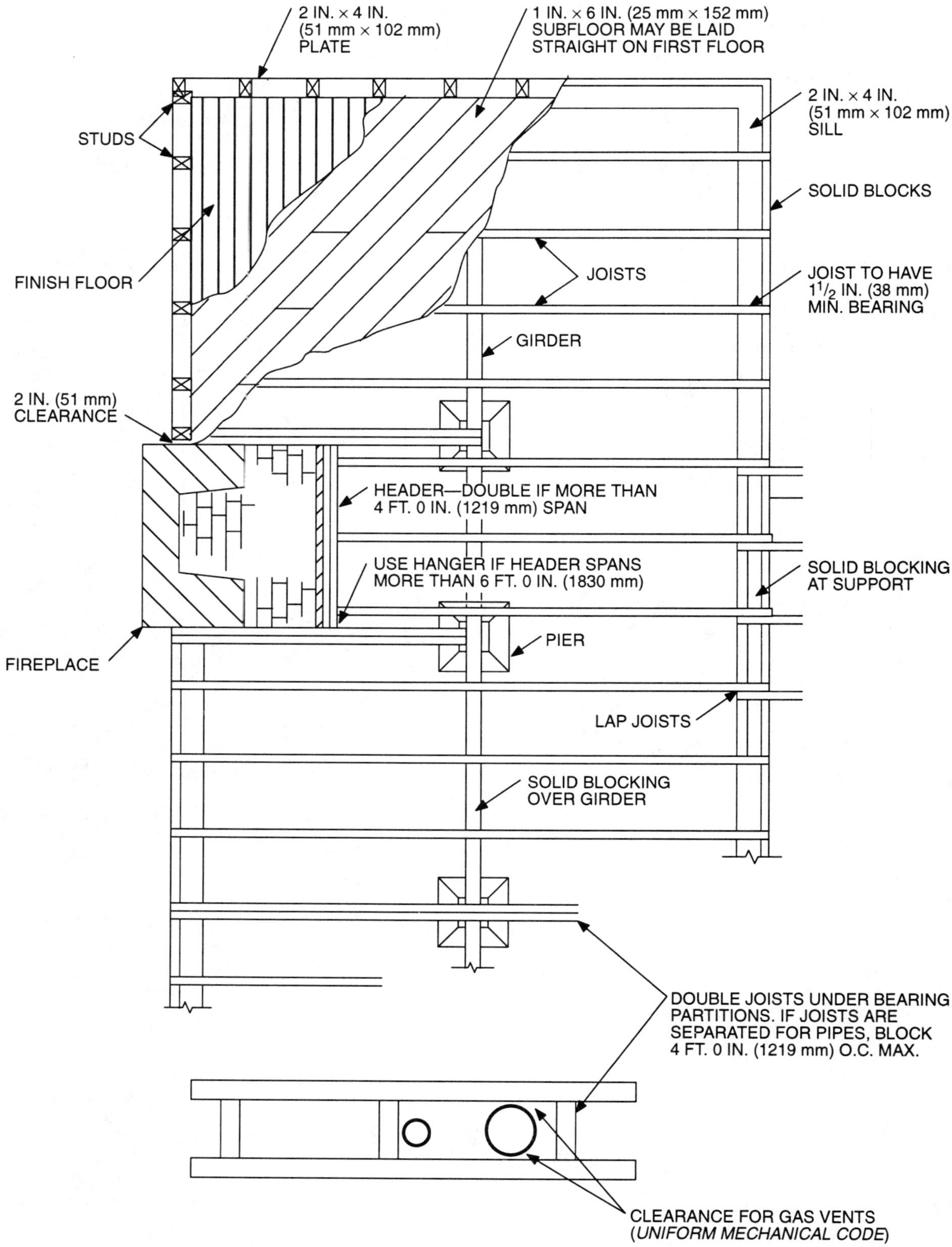

FIGURE 8—FLOOR CONSTRUCTION DETAIL

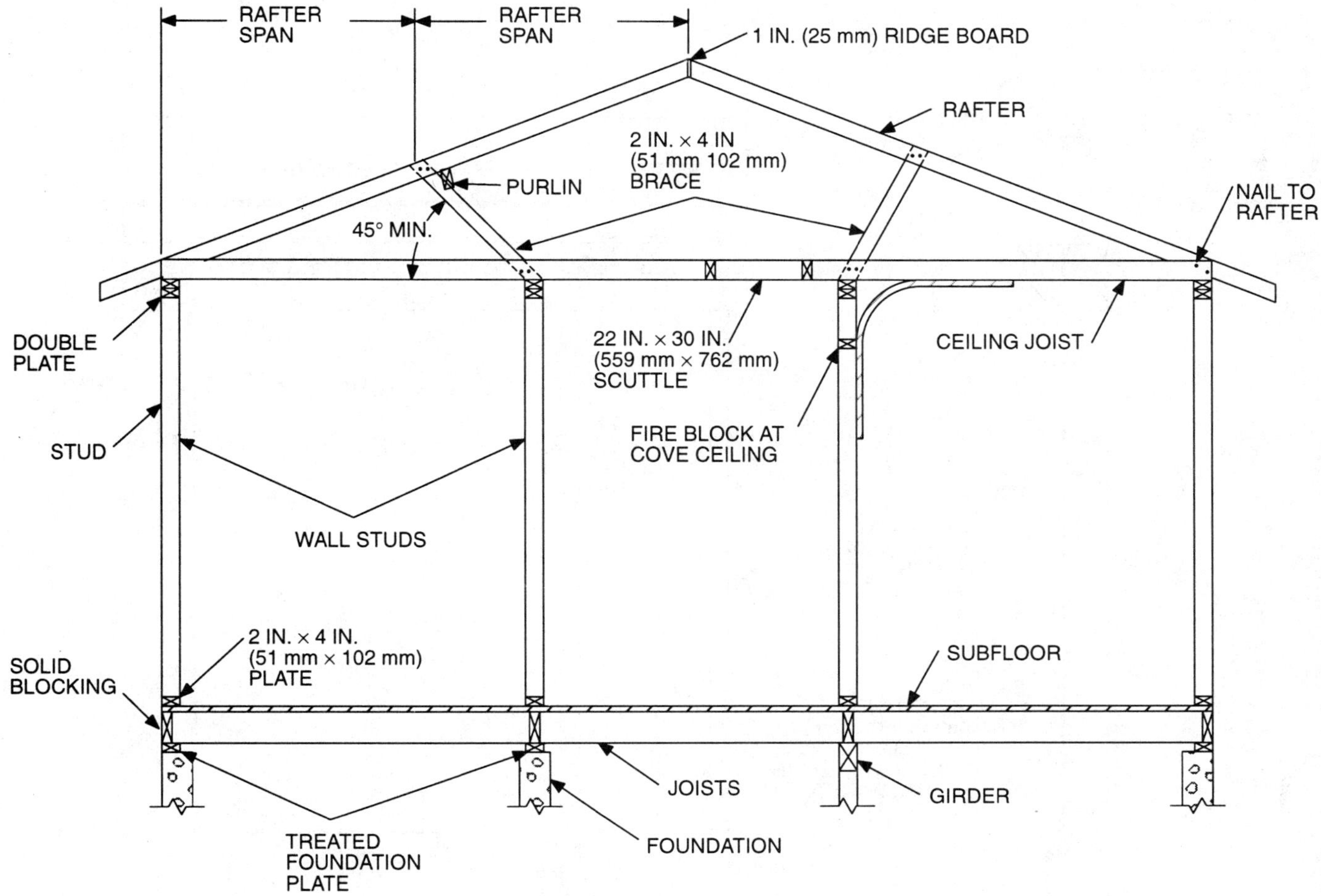

FIGURE 9—ROOF FRAMING DETAIL

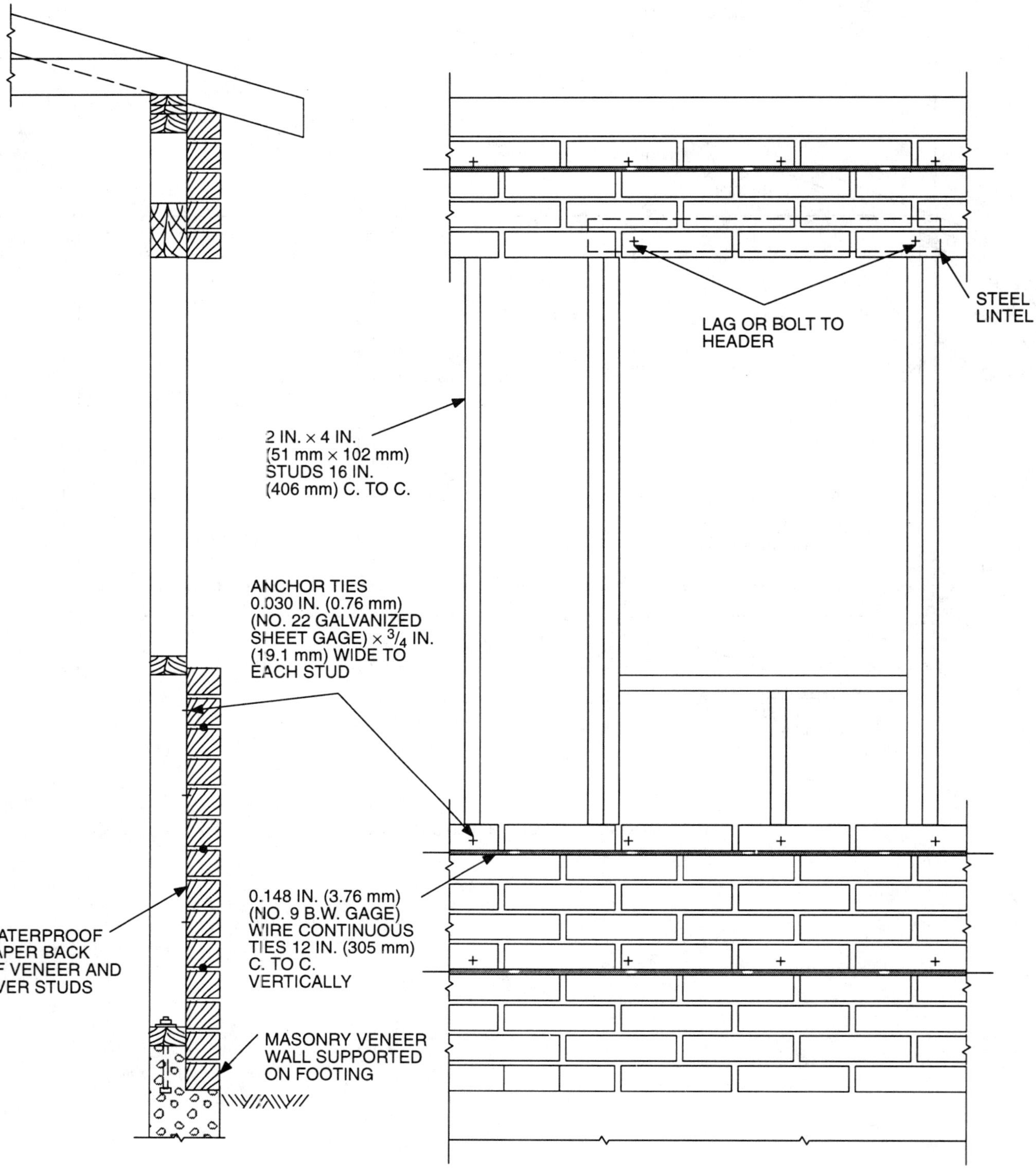

FIGURE 10—MASONRY VENEERED WALL

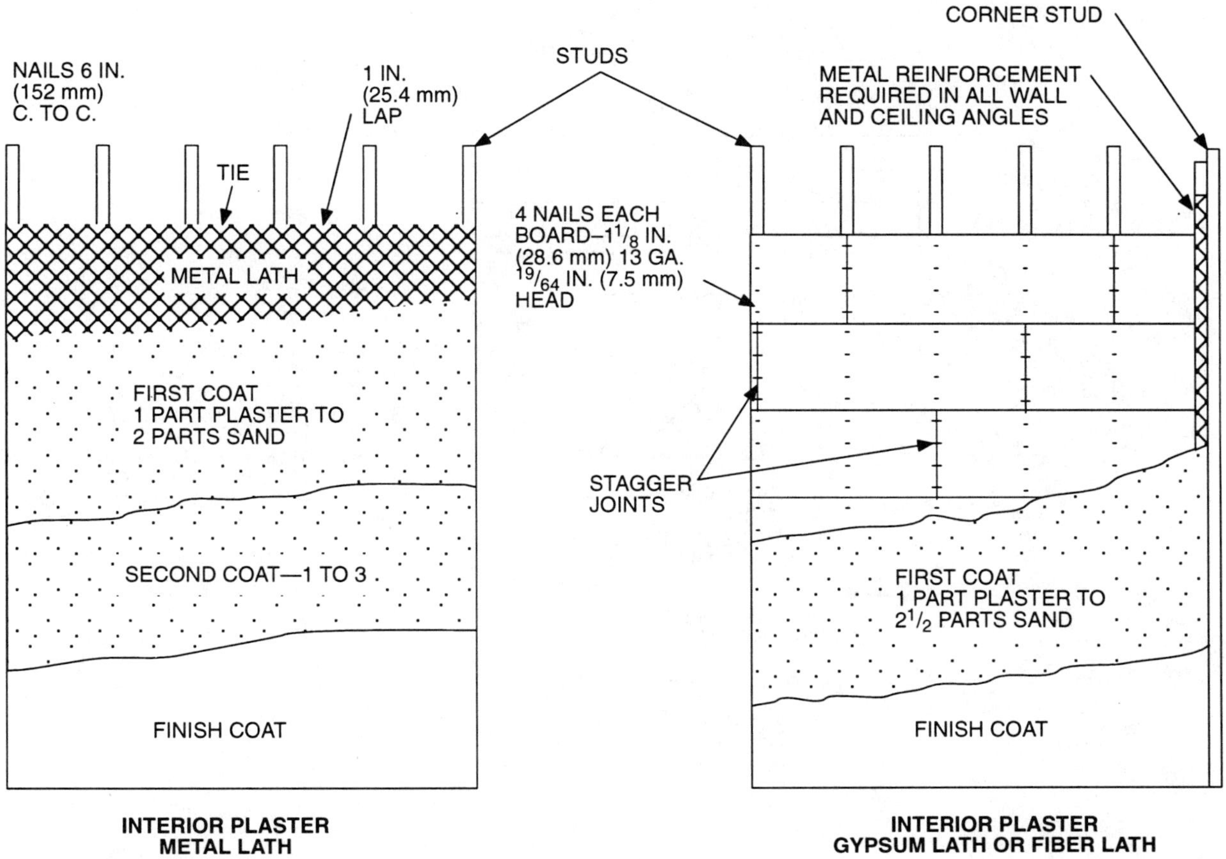

FIGURE 11—INTERIOR PLASTERING DETAIL

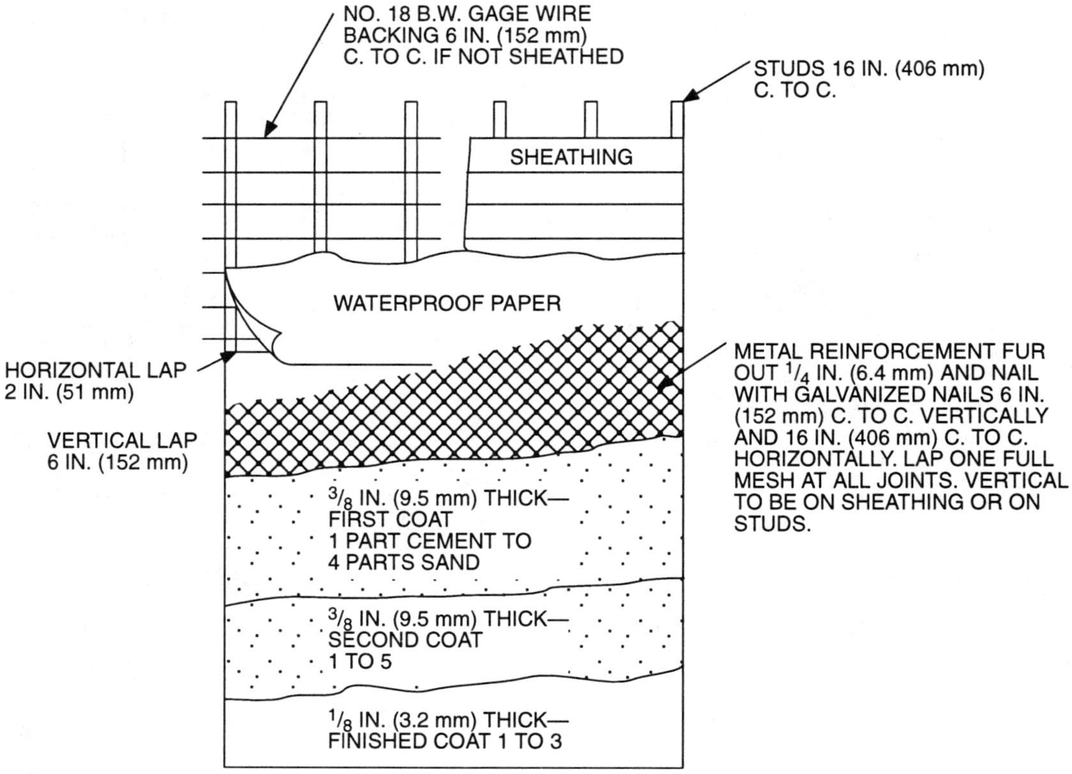

FIGURE 12—EXTERIOR PLASTERING DETAIL